the new vegan

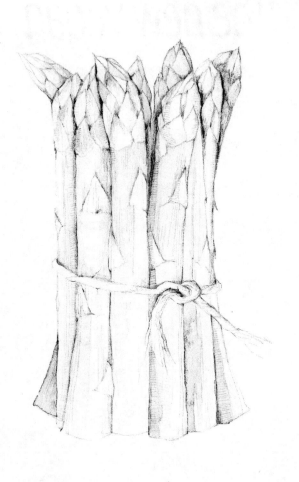

the new vegan

Fresh and exciting recipes
for a healthy lifestyle

Amanda Grant

metro

First published in Great Britain in 1999
by Metro Books (an imprint of Metro Publishing Limited),
19 Gerrard Street, London W1V 7LA

Edited by Tessa Clark
Illustrations by Nicola Cunningham
Cover photographs by David Loftus

British Library Cataloguing in Publication Data.
A CIP record of this book is available on request from the
British Library.

ISBN 1 900512 53 X

10 9 8 7 6 5 4 3 2 1

Typeset by SX Composing DTP, Rayleigh, Essex

Printed in Great Britain by CPD Group, Wales

Contents

1
Introduction

1
Why Vegan?

3
The Vegan Diet and Nutrition

6
Essential Ingredients

13
Starters

57
Snacks & Light Meals

97
Main Courses

151
Desserts

187
Menus

193
Index

Introduction

WHY VEGAN?

What an exciting challenge – writing a book of recipes that are vegetarian and free from dairy produce. The vegan diet is based on a wonderful variety of vegetables, fruits, nuts and seeds, grains and pulses, seasoned with fresh herbs and exotic spices from all over the world. It is a diet that avoids all meat, fish, poultry, animal milk, honey and all products and by-products derived from animals.

I am not exclusively vegan but I believe passionately in the benefits of eating the foods that make up a vegan diet for achieving optimum health and vitality. I also have personal reasons for writing this cookbook and encouraging others to incorporate vegan recipes into their everyday eating.

My background is food- and nutrition-based and I have always had a passion for food, so it would seem logical that I write on this subject. However, my reasons for writing this book are far more important to me. I have spent a number of years researching diet and health with particular interest in cancer and food. My late mother suffered a long, hard-fought battle against cancer; she died in April 1997 after intensive chemotherapy treatment. It is in her memory that I write this book.

There is so much evidence that diet and health are linked, particularly with reference to life-threatening diseases. We are continually being encouraged to increase our consumption of the basic ingredients that constitute a vegan diet, namely fruits and vegetables. The joy that my new recipe ideas gave my mother made me realize that there must be other people who will also take delight in this creativity. Many people seem to suffer from food intolerance in some form, often linked to dairy foods or meat, making it difficult for them to know what to eat and how to make their diets interesting. I see this challenge to create a number of inspirational recipes suitable for vegans as an excellent opportunity to share my background in nutrition and my own love for the subject of food and health.

I normally write quick, fashionable and easy recipes that are influenced by world cuisine, a job that is made so much easier by the fabulous, continuously evolving array of international ingredients available in supermarkets and local shops, particularly the foods of Japan and Morocco. The addition of some hot 'wasabi' (Japanese horseradish), or a sprinkling of thinly sliced pickled ginger over a light noodle dish is tastebud-tingling stuff! Other Japanese ingredients like dashi-konbu, a kind of seaweed, and sake also feature in my recipes. Couscous, one of Morocco's gifts to the culinary world, plays a big role in this book. Having spent much time in France, Italy and Spain, I am also a great fan of the Mediterranean style of cooking, and these cuisines also influence the recipes in the chapters that follow.

I have spent a number of months developing a range of quick, simple but delicious recipes that may help you to live a healthy life and feel great, with more energy and vitality. I think it is important that both ardent carnivores and vegans alike take pleasure in dipping into this book and enjoy all the recipes. Only a few weeks ago, I had a few meat-eating friends around for supper and served a completely vegan menu: all plates were licked clean and there were requests for recipes from everyone. One guest even went so far as to comment on the fact that he had not missed the meat. I know it was only one meal, but it is a start.

It is a complete myth that a diet without meat and dairy produce is dull or monotonous – but meals must be well balanced. Even when you entertain friends who do not share your interest in diet, serving a vegan meal is not a problem. However, it is important to plan a menu that is satisfying, especially when feeding hungry meat-eating males. For those of you who find meal planning a struggle, or just want someone else to do the thinking for you, I have included menus at the end of the book.

I have outlined my reasons for encouraging everyone to eat vegetable-based meals in an everyday diet, but there are many reasons why people are drawn to a vegan way of life. Research shows that 60 per cent of the estimated quarter of a million vegans in the United Kingdom chose the diet on the basis of animal rights issues. This is followed closely by concern for the environment – global warming and the use of land, energy and water. Many people argue that using land for animal farming is inefficient in comparison with plant cultivation. A third of the grain we grow is fed to animals. A vegan diet requires an eighth of the land that is needed to provide food for a meat-based one and there is a strong belief that much of the world food problem could be alleviated if land currently devoted to animal farming was turned over to plant cultivation. Health comes a close third. Interestingly, there is a national campaign to increase our consumption of fruit and vegetables by 25 per cent by 2008. Nutritional targets have been set to encourage us to eat at least five 80g (3oz) portions of fruit and vegetables daily. This speaks volumes for the virtues of a diet based on these ingredients.

Finally, there is a minority of people who have changed to a vegan diet for spiritual reasons. They are reported to experience strong benefits.

Remember that vegan food can be fresh and fast. It does not need to be focused on fancy nut loaves that demand five hours' preparation, plus a similar cooking time. The recipes in this book illustrate the fact that vegan food can be new and creative – or based on established favourites, like lasagne. Contrary to popular belief, vegans do not have to miss out. You can eat cake along with the rest of the party. Just knock up my Chocolate Raspberry Hazelnut Cake (see page 181) – and enjoy.

THE VEGAN DIET AND NUTRITION

There is increasing evidence that both vegan and vegetarian diets can help reduce our chances of cancer, heart disease and stroke as well as diabetes, obesity, varicose veins, piles, gallstones and constipation. This information alone was enough for me to study the subject and to ensure that I eat a lot of vegan meals and encourage my friends and family to do the same. Eating the right vegan foods simply means enjoying fresh, natural, organic and, where possible, raw produce rather than highly processed and refined foods.

An essentially wholefood diet free of animal products is low in cholesterol, high in fibre, high in vitamins and minerals, low in saturated fat and, with a modest intake of sodium, or salt, it fulfils all human nutritional requirements. It is also the diet for which our digestive systems are best suited.

There is no need to panic about achieving the correct balance of vegan foods: just eat a good mix of ingredients. The following gives some idea of the sources of the essential nutrients that should be included. Once you understand the basics, incorporating vegan foods into your diet will become second nature.

Vitamins and Minerals

A varied vegan diet will provide a good supply of vitamins and minerals, and there is an endless list of suitable fresh foods that are good sources of these nutrients. In particular, I like to describe fresh raw fruits and vegetables as nature's own vitamin and mineral pills.

A few other food sources worthy of a mention for their nutrient content, specifically the B vitamins, include almonds, cashew nuts, pecans, pine nuts, dried apricots and Marmite.

Bean sprouts are a good source. When beans or seeds, such as alfalfa, are sprouted, their nutritional value increases, especially the vitamin C and B complex. Also, amino acids are produced, fats are converted into water-soluble vitamins and their enzyme activity increases. Bean sprouts are easily incorporated into the diet – they are so versatile that you can add them to salads and sandwiches as well as to hot vegetable dishes. There are a wide range of beans and seeds that can be sprouted – have fun sprouting them yourself, or buy from supermarkets or health food shops.

Vitamin B_{12}

In nature, vitamin B_{12} is found in animal products but some non-animal foods are fortified with the vitamin, which can be synthesized on a vegetable base. Some seaweeds and some freshwater algae are sources of vitamin B_{12}. To ensure an adequate supply, vegans need to eat foods that are fortified with this vitamin. It is important to check that the product is free from animal sources of the vitamin: check labels or consult the manufacturer if in doubt; alternatively, The Vegan Society (see page 6) may be able to help. Examples of suitable products include Plamil soya milk, Marmite, Barmene and Tastex. Some breakfast cereals are suitable, as is textured vegetable protein (TVP). Miso, a soya bean paste, also contains vitamin B_{12}.

Vitamin D

The other vitamin that needs to be mentioned is vitamin D, which is found in soya milk and fortified foods like cereals; always check the manufacturer's label to ensure that an animal-free source of the vitamin has been used as a supplement. The most significant supply comes from sunlight, which incidentally does not need to be bright. Most people, including infants, require little or no extra vitamin D from food.

Iron

Too little iron in the diet is often a cause of concern as it can lead to anaemia. Good sources of the mineral include whole grains, pumpkin and sesame seeds, nuts (cashew nuts, walnuts, hazelnuts, brazil nuts, pecans and peanuts), green beans, seaweed, dried fruits, molasses, chick peas and red kidney beans. Green leafy vegetables such as spinach and watercress contain a lot of iron, but they also contain oxalic acid, which binds the iron and makes a large proportion of it unavailable to the body. The exciting news is that research shows that, generally, vegans have a high dietary iron intake. Although iron from plant sources is less well absorbed than that from meat, high levels of vitamin C in the diet enhance iron absorption. Studies show that the iron status of vegans is usually normal and that iron deficiency is no more common among them than in the general population.

Eating foods rich in vitamin C at the same time as those that contain iron helps to improve the absorption of the vitamin in the body, ensuring that the available iron is utilized to its full potential. For example, try fruit juice (a good source of vitamin C) instead of soya milk on a nutty muesli (a good source of iron).

Calcium

It is a misconception that cow's milk is the greatest source of calcium. People are often surprised to learn that the mineral is found in leafy green vegetables such as watercress, spinach, pak choi and kale. Fennel, leeks, broccoli, figs, sesame seeds, almonds, brazil nuts, soya milks (Provamel, Plamil and Granovita), tahini (sesame seed paste), figs, seaweed and molasses are all sources of calcium. A cupful of broccoli contains as much calcium as 200ml (7fl oz) milk. I was delighted to read that some research shows that vegans and vegetarians tend to store and use calcium far more efficiently than people who eat meat.

Carbohydrates

Carbohydrates – starches and sugars – provide most of the body's energy. Good sources include bananas, breads, cereals, pasta, potatoes, fruit and vegetables. Refined sugars and lots of sugary snacks are foods to avoid.

Fat

The most obvious sources of fat include oils, seeds, nuts (and nut creams), grains and soya products.

Proteins

Protein deficiency is virtually impossible if we eat sufficient calories to meet our needs. This even applies to children fed a vegan diet: provided their energy needs are met, they thrive on a diet in which protein comes from a mixture of plant foods, and are recorded as being within the normal ranges of height and weight.

Soya products are a great source of protein for vegans. Soya protein is equivalent in value to animal protein. Grains and grain products (wheat, oats, rice, barley, buckwheat, millet, pasta, bread), peas, seeds – I use a lot of pumpkin and sesame seeds in the book – nuts (brazil nuts, hazelnuts, almonds, cashew nuts), yeast, wheatgerm, dried or canned beans like red kidney and cannellini beans and lentils are also good.

As with most nutrients, the best way to consume the right amount is to eat a variety of foods. For example, try a mixture of nuts and seeds for a snack or sprinkle them on salads; eat bean dishes with bread to combine vegetable and wheat proteins. Cannellini beans and olives are good with fresh Italian bread for lunch, or try a chick-pea dip with toasted pitta bread; for supper have a rice dish with a handful of nuts scattered over the top. This provides a good range of foods in one day.

ESSENTIAL INGREDIENTS

I hope the recipes in this book will show that it is relatively easy to cook and enjoy a varied vegan diet without having to spend hours in the kitchen. Similarly, you do not need to buy lots of unusual ingredients. The basics are available from most good supermarkets or health-food shops. Wherever possible, buy fruits and vegetables in season – they are cheaper and often have much more flavour.

The Animal Free Shopper lists products that are suitable for vegans and is available from The Vegan Society, 7 Battle Road, St Leonards on Sea, East Sussex TN37 7AA.

Stocking the Storecupboard

Cans

Apart from beans and pulses, only three ingredients work well in cans. Coconut milk is one of them. It is not the liquid inside a coconut but is made from the grated flesh of fresh coconut. It is normally unsweetened and I tend to use the milk more often than the cream, which is pressed coconut with a thick, creamy texture and which is made with stabilizers and emulsifiers as well as water. The other two ingredients are sweetcorn and tomatoes, especially chopped plum tomatoes without added herbs or garlic.

Dried fruits

Dates, figs, apricots and raisins are delicious mixed into couscous- or rice-based dishes, or added to Moroccan-style chick-pea stews. They are also excellent in puddings or for making sauces – puréed apricots with orange juice makes a wonderful sauce. Pack a few dried fruits into your lunchbox and nibble on these instead of crisps.

Grains

Keep couscous, polenta, soya flour, porridge oats and, if you wish, a packet of bulghur (cracked wheat) in the storecupboard. I tend to prefer couscous to bulghur. It is just as easy to use. Cover the grains in a warm stock and leave to soak for at least 15 minutes, until all the liquid has been absorbed, add lots of herbs, olive oil and a few roasted vegetables and you have a fabulous supper dish.

Jams

Buy fruit jams with a high fruit content and little sugar. They are great added to soya yogurt or custards made with vegan powder and spread thickly on scones or fruit breads.

Nuts and seeds

Pumpkin and sunflower seeds are delicious toasted and tossed over vegetable dishes or salads. A handful of nuts (especially almonds, cashew nuts or brazil nuts) toasted and tossed in olive oil is always a quick treat. Both nuts and seeds transform rice dishes and hot vegetables into a complete meal.

Nut spreads

There are many to choose from in the shops. Tahini (made from sesame seeds), peanut butter and cashew nut butter are my favourites. They can be spread on biscuits or bread for a quick snack and peanut butter can be used to make a satay sauce (see Spicy Satay on White Bread, page 88).

Oils

Keep a light olive oil and an extra virgin one in the storecupboard. The latter is great for salad dressings and drizzling over lightly cooked vegetables or finished dishes – or drizzled on fresh bread that has been rubbed with garlic. If you have room in the cupboard, also go for a bland groundnut (peanut) oil for frying and the faithful walnut oil for salad dressings – just mix it with a little lemon or lime juice. Sesame oil is strong in flavour so you will only use a little at a time, and is great for drizzling over stir-fries or noodles.

Pasta

Keep a few favourites in the storecupboard. Most varieties of pasta, including gnocchi, are made with or without eggs, so check the list of ingredients on the packet to make sure that eggs have been omitted.

Pulses

Chick peas, cannellini beans, kidney beans, butter beans, broad beans, puy lentils and green lentils are my favourites. Most of my recipes use canned varieties that require no soaking and precooking. Simply give them a good rinse under the tap to remove the sugar or salt that is often found in their water.

Rice

Basmati, Thai jasmine rice, Japanese sushi rice, arborio (or other risotto rice) and pudding rice all feature in the book. Thai jasmine rice is a delicately flavoured long grain rice that is perfect with coconut or Thai-based curries. The grains of sushi rice, which comes mainly from California, are small, plump and often slightly soft and squidgy when cooked. It needs to be dressed with a vinegar and sugar solution while it is still warm so that it absorbs the dressing as it cools.

Salt

Maldon sea salt flakes have such a wonderful taste of the sea that you will add less salt than normal to your food.

Sauces and pastes

Chutneys, whole-grain mustards, olive pastes, pesto and soy sauce are essentials. So is harissa, the North African chilli paste that can transform couscous recipes in seconds. Always check the ingredients list to make sure the sauce doesn't contain animal products. Rustica crushed tomatoes are not strictly a sauce or paste – but are also an essential.

Seaweed

This provides an excellent source of vitamins A, C, D, E and K plus B vitamins, including B_{12}, which as I mentioned earlier is a vitamin that is rarely present in vegetables grown on land. It is also rich in minerals, especially iron. Dashi-konbu is great for adding a sweet flavour to rice. Nori is brilliant for wrapping around rice – you could adapt the Vegan Sushi with Avocado and Cucumber (see page 107) and wrap nori around the rice balls. Alternatively, next time you are near a Japanese store pick up a packet of seaweed and add some to a vegetable stir-fry.

Spices
Keep a few whole spices like green cardamom pods, coriander seeds, black peppercorns, cinnamon sticks, nutmeg and dried chillies in the store-cupboard and grind them as and when required. Other spices worth keeping are star anise and vanilla pods or extract – the recipe for Fruits with Cardomom and Vanilla on page 159 makes use of their full potential. Always use an extract of vanilla – which is the real thing – rather than vanilla essence, which is artificial. And don't forget saffron, a pretty and tasty friend. Chilli powder also features in many of my recipes. There are lots of different ones to choose from, but I strongly recommend Kashmiri chilli powder, which has an excellent flavour and heat. Quick tip: add dried orange or lime zest to your pepper mill for a wonderfully fresh seasoning.

Sugars
Unrefined sugars – soft light or dark brown sugars, golden caster sugar and golden icing sugar – are the only ones to use. They lock in the natural molasses of sugar cane rather than refining it out and once you have used them you will never cook with any other kind. My favourite is light soft brown sugar, which adds a touch of fudge to anything it touches. Look out for Billingtons, or for own-label brands (but check that the label says 'unrefined' as you may otherwise buy a white sugar that has been coloured brown).

Vegetable stock
Homemade is best but, failing that, Swiss vegetable vegan bouillon powder is made with only organic products, including yeast extract, dried onions, dried carrots and dried parsley, and is widely available in supermarkets.

Vinegars
Balsamic vinegar is essential but you will have to spend a little bit of cash in order to get one with a good dark, sweet and rich, mellow flavour. Rice wine vinegar is also essential. It once took time and patience to find this little ingredient, now all you need do is pop into the nearest supermarket. Cider and red wine vinegar are both useful, but not essential.

Stocking the Fridge
If you have a number of key ingredients in the fridge, you will always be able to whip up a quick meal, whether it is a pasta dish with chillies, ginger and herbs, or a salsa spread on part-baked bread and transformed into a pizza.

Chillies

A general guide is that long, thin chillies are hotter than those with broad shoulders, but the medium-sized box-shaped Scotch bonnet proves otherwise, so when a recipe calls for chillies just add a little at a time and taste as you go along – you can always add more. As soon as you add an ingredient like coconut milk or any other high-fat liquid the taste will become milder. Fresh chillies with wrinkled skins are hotter than the smooth kind. Dried chillies are the exact opposite: wrinkled ones are often sweeter than smooth ones.

Ginger

This knobbly root will keep for several weeks in the vegetable drawer. Wrap it in kitchen paper and pop it into a paper bag.

Herbs

I've used fresh herbs in all my recipes – a handful scattered over a dish adds so much colour and flavour. If you can grow herbs, do.

Lemon grass

This is a staple of South-east Asian cooking. Remember to bash the thin end of the stick before using as this helps to release its citrus flavour.

Lemons and limes

Cut the fruit into chunks and griddle or fry them until golden. Serve alongside a vegetable or pasta dish.

Salsa

You will never be caught short if you have part-baked bread in your freezer and a good-quality salsa in your fridge – at the least you will be able to make a homemade pizza.

Soya milk and soya cream

Many different brands are available. Try a variety and decide which ones you prefer.

Vegan margarine

There are many brands of margarine, all basically made from vegetable oils. But remember to check the label to make sure a margarine does not contain gelatine, whey, caseinates or other products derived from animals.

Vegetables
Leafy green vegetables – a packet of spinach leaves or bag of pak choi – are useful standbys. Choose organic produce whenever possible.

Stocking the Freezer
I love my freezer – I can always dip into it and find something to turn into supper. The following are my essentials – but I always like to leave room for homemade shortcakes (see page 78).

Berries
Whiz some berries in a food processor with soya ice-cream or yogurt or crush the berries and mix them with a sorbet. Serve in wine glasses.

Loaf of part-baked bread
Whoever pops in unexpectedly will be more than happy when they smell it baking – and even more delighted to taste fresh, squidgy bread topped with a little garlic and a drizzle of olive oil.

Sorbets and ice-creams
There are many good fruit sorbets. Look for one with a high fruit content and check the label to make sure it doesn't contain products derived from animals. My favourite ice-cream is Soyice, which is almost indistinguishable from traditional ice-creams.

Young broad beans or petits pois
If you don't have time to buy vegetables on your way home, you will at least have something sweet and green on your plate for supper.

Pastry
Jus-Rol vegan puff and shortcrust pastry, and filo pastry are freezer essentials. Seriously, who would make any of these from scratch when ready-made versions are available?

Some extra ingredients
These seem slightly too indulgent to be described as essentials.

Kaffir lime leaves

There is something almost magical about these leaves. They do not have the strong citric flavour of lime juice but are more aromatic. Experiment with them: throw a couple into the water when you are cooking rice or pasta, or a curry that uses lemon grass.

Pickled ginger

This wonderful Japanese ingredient adds a kick to food and is also decorative. Avoid the bright pink kind – the colour indicates the presence of a nasty dye.

Wasabi

This may look like toothpaste in its squeezy tube, but don't be fooled. Put it in a little bowl and use with caution. It is Japanese horseradish and has real attitude.

Wines and spirits

A few bottles of white and red wine and a couple of liqueurs for those fruit desserts are good storecupboard ingredients. Check the lists provided by The Vegan Society for varieties and stockists: animal-derived products are often used in the production of alcoholic beverages, in the fining or clearing process or as colorants and anti-foaming agents. Most spirits are acceptable (with the exception of malt whisky, some blended whiskies and Spanish brandies). I use a selection of spirits and organic wine in my recipes.

A note on honey

Because bees produce honey it could be classed as an animal food. However, some vegans argue that making it does not cause any harm to the bees. The arguments for and against have caused disagreements and some vegans use honey, others do not. I have not used honey in the recipes in this book.

Spiced Nuts

This is a quick and easy nibble for serving with drinks. I was inspired to create the recipe after eating in an American restaurant where the chef had scattered something similar to these spicy nuts over a crisp green salad. The quantity is quite large – deliberately. Any left-over nuts will keep for up to three weeks in a screw-top jar and are perfect for satisfying hunger pangs or pepping up green salads or vegetables. Check the 'hotness' of the nuts when they have cooled. If they are not spicy enough for you, heat a little more oil, add more chilli powder then return the nuts to the frying pan and cook them for a few minutes, tossing them to prevent them burning.

Serves 6 (approx.)
Preparation time: 5 minutes
Cooking time: 5 minutes

1 tablespoon vegetable oil

1–2 teaspoons chilli powder, preferably Kashmiri chilli powder

mixed nuts, about 300g (10½oz) total; I recommend brazil nuts and almonds

3–4 tablespoons soy sauce

Maldon salt

◆ Heat the oil in a wok or large frying pan. Add the chilli powder and cook, stirring, over a high heat for 1 minute. Add the nuts and toss them in the oil and chilli powder until they are well coated. Fry the nuts for 1 minute, tossing and turning them as you do so.

◆ Add the soy sauce to the frying pan – it will sizzle as it hits the hot nuts. Cook over a high heat for 3 minutes or until all the sauce has evaporated, stirring frequently so that the nuts do not burn.

◆ Scatter a little salt over the nuts and then spread them on kitchen paper to drain and cool.

EACH SERVING CONTAINS
Kcals 345 • Protein 9g • Fat 32g (of which saturated 5.5g) • Carbohydrate 3g • Fibre 3g
Kcals from fat 86% • Excellent source of vitamin E

Coriander Spiced Nuts

*These make a wonderful change to a bowl of plain nuts and there is
something virtuous about saying that you made them. Whenever you
use nuts in a recipe they should ideally be roasted or dry-fried to give
the finished dish a really good nutty flavour. These ones can be stored
in a jar for up to three weeks – make sure it is airtight or the nuts will
go soft.*

Serves 4
Preparation time: 10 minutes
Cooking time: 10–15 minutes

170g (6oz) sesame seeds

50g (1¾oz) coriander seeds

50g (1¾oz) hazelnuts

50g (1¾oz) cashew nuts

**Maldon salt and freshly ground
black pepper**

◆ Preheat the oven to 180°C/350°F/Gas 4. Dry-fry the sesame seeds and
coriander seeds over a moderate heat in a heavy-based frying pan, turning
or stirring frequently, for about 5 minutes until the seeds are golden and
starting to pop. Coarsely crush them using a pestle and mortar.

◆ Spread out the hazelnuts and cashew nuts on a baking tray and roast for
10–15 minutes until golden all over. Rub the skins off the hazelnuts.
Coarsely chop all the nuts.

◆ Mix the nuts and seeds together, season with salt and pepper and serve.

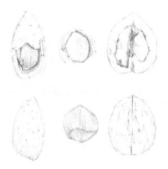

EACH SERVING CONTAINS
Kcals 410 • Protein 12g • Fat 39g (of which saturated 5g) • Carbohydrate 3g • Fibre 4.5g
Kcals from fat 85% • Good source of vitamin E

Hot and Spicy Popcorn

It is important to use a heavy-based saucepan or frying pan to prevent the popcorn from burning. A tight-fitting lid is also essential to ensure that the corn stays in the pan until all of it has popped. If you prefer a sweeter version, add a sweet spice like cinnamon instead of cayenne and paprika, and replace the salt with a sprinkle of sugar. Serve the popcorn with drinks, or cool it and keep it in an airtight container until you are in the mood for a quick snack.

Serves 4
Preparation time: 5 minutes
Cooking time: 10–15 minutes

1 tablespoon vegetable oil

85g (3oz) corn kernels

2 tablespoons olive oil

pinch of cayenne pepper

pinch of paprika

Maldon salt and freshly ground black pepper

◆ Heat the vegetable oil in a heavy-based saucepan or frying pan until it starts to shimmer. Add enough corn kernels to form a single layer. Cover the pan. Listen carefully and when the kernels begin to pop, turn the heat down and shake the pan gently every now and then. When the popping stops, take the pan off the heat and tip the popcorn into a dish. Repeat with the remaining corn kernels.

◆ Toss the popcorn with the olive oil until well coated, and sprinkle with the cayenne pepper, paprika and salt and pepper to taste. Serve warm or cold.

EACH SERVING CONTAINS
Kcals 94 • Protein 1g • Fat 9g (of which saturated 1g) • Carbohydrate 3g
Fibre 0.3g • Kcals from fat 82%

Roasted Baby Courgettes

An unusual nibble to serve with drinks. If baby courgettes are unavailable, use the same quantity of large ones and slice the cooked vegetables before serving.

Serves 4
Preparation time: 15 minutes
Cooking time: 15 minutes

400g (14oz) baby courgettes

75g (2½oz) almonds

75g (2½oz) white breadcrumbs

1 tablespoon extra virgin olive oil

Maldon salt and freshly ground black pepper

◆ Preheat the oven to 200°C/400°F/Gas 6. Slice the courgettes in half lengthways and scoop out their seeds with a teaspoon.

◆ Dry-fry the almonds in a heavy-based frying pan over a moderate heat, turning or stirring frequently, for 5 minutes or until they are golden.

◆ Put the almonds and breadcrumbs in a bowl, season well with salt and pepper and mix thoroughly. Spoon the mixture into the courgette halves, packing it in as tightly as possible, and drizzle the olive oil over them. Bake in the oven for 15 minutes. If you want the filling to look more golden, put the courgettes under a preheated grill for 2 minutes. Serve hot.

Olives with Fresh Rosemary and Orange

Olives are always popular accompaniments to drinks and presented this way they look delicious – and are very quick to prepare. The longer you can leave them to marinate the better. Leave out the garlic if you want the olives to have a subtle herb and citrus flavour. The strips of orange zest should be thick so that you can avoid them easily when serving.

Serves 4
Preparation time: 5 minutes, plus at least 1 hour marinating time

250g (9oz) mixed black and green olives, with pits

2 thick strips orange zest

3–4 sprigs of fresh rosemary

handful of fresh flat-leaf parsley, roughly chopped

1 garlic clove, sliced (optional)

3 tablespoons extra virgin olive oil

◆ Mix all the ingredients together in a serving bowl and leave to marinate for at least 1 hour.

◆ Remove the rosemary sprigs and orange zest.

EACH SERVING CONTAINS
Kcals 140 • Protein 0.5g • Fat 15g (of which saturated 2g)
Fibre 2g • Kcals from fat 98%

Puréed Avocado Dip with Pickled Ginger and Wasabi

In the tropics the soft, lovely lime-green flesh of the avocado is known as 'poor man's butter'. The Hass variety is definitely my favourite. When ripe it is black and knobbly on the exterior with a dense-textured flesh that has a nutty – almost hazelnut-like – flavour. Avocados tend to discolour if they are prepared too far in advance, so get all the ingredients for this recipe ready and prepare it just before you want to serve the dip. Two Japanese ingredients – pickled ginger and wasabi paste – add a kick. Serve with crudités and a bowl of the pickled ginger.

Serves 4
Preparation time: 15 minutes

---

3 large ripe avocados (preferably Hass)

2 tablespoons sweet pickled ginger

1 teaspoon wasabi paste

2 spring onions, trimmed and finely sliced

2 tablespoons sesame seeds

Maldon salt and freshly ground black pepper

1 tablespoon sunflower seeds

◆ Slice each avocado in half lengthways and remove the stone. Use a teaspoon to scoop the flesh into a small bowl. Add the pickled ginger, wasabi paste, spring onions and sesame seeds. Mash everything together and season with salt and pepper.

◆ Spoon the dip into a serving bowl and scatter the sunflower seeds over the top. Serve immediately.

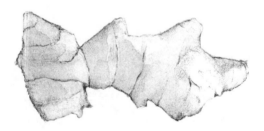

EACH SERVING CONTAINS
Kcals 305 • Protein 4g • Fat 31g (of which saturated 7g) • Carbohydrate 2g
Fibre 5g • Kcals from fat 92% • Good source of vitamins C and E

Lemon Tahini Dip

Tahini is a paste made from sesame seeds. Dips like this one are often served with Middle Eastern dishes like falafel. The cumin seeds in this recipe are dry-fried and, as with all spices, this really enhances their flavour. I enjoy this dip spread on slices of fresh ripe plum tomato or with hot griddled vegetables (see page 31). It is also delicious served with pitta toasts (see page 30). Add more than 1 teaspoon harissa paste if you wish – the more you add, the hotter the dip gets. The dip will keep for up to two days in the fridge.

Serves 4
Preparation time: 15 minutes
Cooking time: 5 minutes

1 teaspoon cumin seeds

50g (1¾oz) tahini

juice of 1 lemon

1 teaspoon harissa

120ml (4fl oz) boiling water

Maldon salt and freshly ground
black pepper

◆ Dry-fry the cumin seeds in a heavy-based frying pan over a moderate heat, turning or stirring frequently, for 3–4 minutes until golden. Coarsely crush the seeds using a pestle and mortar.

◆ Put the cumin in a bowl with the tahini, lemon juice, harissa and salt and pepper. Pour the boiling water over the mixture. Whisk thoroughly with a fork until well mixed. Cover the bowl with cling film and chill before serving.

EACH SERVING CONTAINS
Kcals 76 • Protein 2g • Fat 7g (of which saturated 1g)
Carbohydrate 0g • Fibre 1g • Kcals from fat 88%

Vegetable Crisps

A very easy start to a meal. Big bowls of vegetable crisps look great, taste delicious and are very simple to make. Use a vegetable peeler or sharp knife to cut the vegetables into the thinnest possible slices – aim for 'potato crisp' size.

Serves 4
Preparation time: 20 minutes
Cooking time: about 25 minutes

vegetable oil, for deep-frying
200g (7oz) parsnips, thinly sliced
450g (1lb) sweet potatoes, peeled and thinly sliced

450g (1lb) raw beetroot, peeled and thinly sliced
Maldon salt
cayenne pepper (optional)

♦ Preheat the oven to 150°C/300°F/Gas 2. Line a plate or baking tray with kitchen paper. Half-fill a deep-fryer or heavy-based deep saucepan with the vegetable oil and heat to 190°C (375°F). To test the temperature, drop a cube of bread in the oil – it should brown within seconds.

♦ Carefully drop a handful of vegetable slices into the oil and fry for 3–4 minutes until they are golden and crisp. Remove the slices with a slotted spoon, drain them on the kitchen paper, then transfer them to the oven to keep warm. If you put too many vegetables into the oil at one time, the temperature of the oil will be lowered and the crisps will be greasy and soggy when cooked.

♦ Repeat the process with the remaining vegetable slices.

♦ Transfer the crisps to a warm serving dish, sprinkle salt and cayenne pepper, if using, over them and serve.

EACH SERVING CONTAINS
Kcals 200 • Protein 3g • Fat 10g (of which saturated 1g) • Carbohydrate 26g
Fibre 5g • Kcals from fat 45% • Good source of folic acid, vitamins C, A and E

Cayenne Chips

A bowl of spicy chips is a delicious way to start a casual supper. I fry them for a few minutes, drain them on kitchen paper and then fry them quickly again so that the chips are crisp on the outside and fluffy in the middle.

Serves 4
Preparation time: 15 minutes
Cooking time: about 15 minutes

900g (2lb) potatoes, peeled
8 teaspoons cayenne pepper

vegetable oil, for deep-frying
Maldon salt

◆ Preheat the oven to 150°C/300°F/Gas 2. Line a plate or baking tray with kitchen paper. Cut the potatoes lengthways into 1cm (½in) slices, then cut the slices in half lengthways. Sprinkle 3 teaspoons cayenne pepper over the slices.

◆ Half-fill a deep-fryer or heavy-based deep saucepan with the vegetable oil and heat to 190°C (375°F). To test the temperature, drop a cube of bread in the oil – it should brown within seconds.

◆ Carefully drop half the potato slices into the oil and fry for 4–5 minutes. Remove and spread them out to drain on kitchen paper. Heat the oil to 190°C (375°F) again, then return the chips to the deep-fryer or saucepan for 1 minute. Spread them out on the kitchen paper, sprinkle with 1 teaspoon cayenne pepper and salt to taste, and transfer to the oven to keep warm. Repeat with the remaining potato slices.

◆ Transfer to a warm serving bowl and serve.

EACH SERVING CONTAINS
Kcals 290 • Protein 5g • Fat 14g (of which saturated 1.5g)
Carbohydrate 39g • Fibre 3g • Kcals from fat 43%

Melon with Red Wine and Mint Sauce

The contrast between the melon and the red sauce makes for a visually stunning dish. I like to use a Galia or canteloupe, but any melon in season will be fine provided it is fresh and ripe. Check for this by smelling it – it should have a wonderful aroma. I have used red wine and golden icing sugar for the sauce, but any combination of wine and sugar tends to perk up most fruits. If you are looking for a quick dessert or starter, choose a selection of seasonal fruits, drizzle some white wine and a sprinkling of golden caster sugar over them and serve.

Serves 4
Preparation time: 15 minutes
Cooking time: 10 minutes

100ml (3½fl oz) dry red wine

2 tablespoons golden icing sugar

60ml (2fl oz) red wine vinegar

finely grated zest of 1 orange

large handful of fresh mint leaves, roughly chopped

freshly ground black pepper

1 large ripe melon

handful of fresh mint leaves, to serve

◆ Mix the wine and sugar in a saucepan and heat gently until the sugar has dissolved. Leave to cool.

◆ Stir the vinegar, orange zest and mint into the wine syrup and season to taste with pepper.

◆ Cut the melon in half and scoop out the seeds with a teaspoon. Cut each half lengthways into 2 segments. Slice the flesh away from the skin of each segment by running a knife blade between the flesh and skin and cut the flesh into long thin strips.

◆ Divide the melon strips between 4 plates and drizzle a little of the sauce over them. Add a scattering of mint leaves and serve with any remaining sauce.

EACH SERVING CONTAINS
Kcals 110 • Protein 1g • Fat less than 1g (of which none is saturated) • Carbohydrate 22g
Fibre 1.3g • Kcals from fat 2% • Excellent source of vitamin C

Melon with Toasted Seeds

A Galia or canteloupe melon, or any melon in season, is fine for this recipe. The seeds are also delicious scattered over hot vegetables like Steamed Pak Choi with Soy Sauce and Toasted Seeds (see page 28) or salads. Alternatively, do as I do and nibble on them while sipping a cool drink.

Serves 4
Preparation time: 2 minutes
Cooking time: 8–12 minutes

200g (7oz) pumpkin seeds
50ml (2fl oz) extra virgin olive oil
Maldon salt

freshly ground black pepper
1 Galia melon

◆ Preheat the oven to 180°C/350°F/Gas 4. Mix the pumpkin seeds with the olive oil and spread them on a baking sheet. Scatter a little salt over them and bake for about 10 minutes until lightly toasted. Remove the seeds from the oven, sprinkle with pepper and more salt, and leave to cool.

◆ Cut the melon in half and scoop out the seeds with a teaspoon. Cut each half lengthways into 2 segments. Slice the flesh away from the skin of each segment by running a knife blade between the flesh and skin and cut the flesh into bite-sized chunks.

◆ Divide the melon chunks between 4 plates, scatter the crunchy seasoned seeds over them and serve.

EACH SERVING CONTAINS
Kcals 495 • Protein 13g • Fat 41g (of which saturated 6g) • Carbohydrate 18g
Fibre 3.5g • Kcals from fat 75% • Good source of vitamin C

Chilli Pakoras with Chunky Tomato Chutney

These vegetables fried in batter are crispy, hot and simple to make. The vegetables must be cut into bite-sized pieces so that they are easy to eat – especially important if you wish to serve them as canapés. The water for the batter must be very cold, so put it in the fridge to chill before you start the recipe. Gram flour is also known as chick-pea flour.

Serves 4
Preparation time: 20 minutes
Cooking time: about 20 minutes

---

2 teaspoons cumin seeds

2 teaspoons coriander seeds

2 teaspoons dried chilli flakes

2 tablespoons vegetable oil

170g (6oz) gram flour

2 teaspoons garam masala

1 teaspoon Maldon salt

200ml (7fl oz) chilled water

½ handful of fresh mint leaves,
    roughly chopped

½ handful of coriander leaves,
    roughly chopped

vegetable oil, for deep-frying

550g (1¼lb) mixed vegetables, such
    as mushrooms, cauliflower,
    okra, courgettes, cut into bite-
    sized pieces

Chunky Tomato Chutney (see page
    143)

◆ Preheat the oven to 150°C/300°F/Gas 2. Dry-fry the cumin seeds, coriander seeds and chilli flakes in a heavy-based saucepan over a moderate heat, turning or stirring frequently, for a couple of minutes until the seeds begin to pop. Coarsely crush the spices using a pestle and mortar.

◆ Heat the oil in a frying pan, add the spices and stir-fry them over a moderate heat for 2 minutes to 'cook off' the spice flavour.

◆ Line a plate or baking tray with kitchen paper. Mix the gram flour, garam masala and salt together in a bowl. Mix in the spice mixture, then gradually add chilled water to make a coating batter, beating vigorously with a wooden spoon or a balloon whisk to remove any lumps. Stir in the mint and coriander. Leave the batter to stand for about 30 minutes.

◆ Heat the oil to about 190°C (375°F) in a deep-fryer or deep, heavy-based saucepan. To test the temperature, drop a little batter into the oil – it should sizzle immediately. When the oil is hot enough, dip 3–4 pieces of vegetable in the batter, then put them carefully in the oil and fry for about 4 minutes or until they are golden brown. Drain the slices on the kitchen

---

paper, then transfer them to the oven to keep warm. Repeat the process with the remaining vegetables.

◆ Serve the pakoras hot with a bowl of Chunky Tomato Chutney as an accompaniment.

EACH SERVING CONTAINS
Kcals 215 • Protein 12g • Fat 9g (of which saturated 1g) • Carbohydrate 23g
Fibre 6g • Kcals from fat 36%

Steamed Pak Choi with Soy Sauce and Toasted Seeds

A bowl of steaming soy greens and toasted seeds is an excellent – and simple – way to begin a supper. Don't forget the chopsticks. Pak choi is available in supermarkets. The leaves look a little like spinach and taste delicious raw or quickly cooked.

Serves 4
Preparation time: 15 minutes
Cooking time: 15 minutes

200g (7oz) pumpkin seeds

50ml (2fl oz) extra virgin olive oil

2 heads of pak choi

2 tablespoons groundnut oil

1 tablespoon chopped garlic

2 tablespoons soy sauce

Maldon salt and freshly ground black pepper

◆ Preheat the oven to 180°C/350°F/Gas 4. Mix the pumpkin seeds with the olive oil and spread them on a baking sheet. Scatter a little salt over them and bake for about 10 minutes until lightly toasted. Remove the seeds from the oven, sprinkle with pepper and more salt, and leave to cool.

◆ Slice each head of pak choi down the middle from the top of the leaves to the stalk, then slice each half into thin strips.

◆ Heat the oil in a wok or large frying pan. Add the garlic and fry gently for a few minutes, then stir in the soy sauce. Add the pak choi and toss the strips in the garlic and soy sauce until they are well coated and the pak choi has wilted slightly.

◆ Divide the greens between 4 warm bowls, scatter the toasted seeds over them and serve.

EACH SERVING CONTAINS
Kcals 70 • Protein 2g • Fat 6g (of which saturated 0.6g) • Carbohydrate 2g
Fibre 1g • Kcals from fat 76% • Good source of vitamin C

Vegetables in a Crispy Chick-Pea Batter

The batter will keep for 3–4 days in the fridge – you may need to add just a little water to thin it down slightly before using it. Adding paprika and cayenne just before the vegetables are served looks attractive and gives the batter that extra burst of flavour. You could always serve these crispy vegetables with Chunky Tomato Chutney (see page 143). The water for the batter must be very cold, so put it in the fridge to chill before you start the recipe.

Serves 4
Preparation time: 10 minutes
Cooking time: about 20–30 minutes

200g (7oz) chick-pea flour

1 garlic clove, crushed

2 teaspoons cumin seeds

½ teaspoon turmeric

½ teaspoon baking powder

2 tablespoons olive oil

360ml (12fl oz) chilled water

vegetable oil, for deep-frying

675g (1½lb) mixed fresh
    vegetables, such as broccoli,
    cauliflower and courgettes, cut
    into bite-sized pieces

1 teaspoon cayenne pepper

1 teaspoon paprika

Maldon salt and freshly ground
    black pepper

◆ Preheat the oven to 150°C/300°F/Gas 2. Line a plate or baking tray with kitchen paper. Mix the chick-pea flour, garlic, cumin seeds, turmeric, baking powder and salt and pepper together in a bowl. Mix in the olive oil, then gradually add 360ml (12fl oz) chilled water, or enough to make a coating batter, beating vigorously with a wooden spoon or a balloon whisk to remove any lumps. Leave the batter to stand for about 30 minutes.

◆ Heat the oil to about 180°C (355°F) in a deep-fryer or deep, heavy-based saucepan. To test the temperature, drop a little batter into the oil – it should sizzle immediately. When the oil is hot enough, dip 3–4 pieces of vegetable in the batter, then put them carefully in the oil and fry for about 4 minutes or until they are golden brown. Drain them on the kitchen paper and transfer them to the oven to keep warm. Repeat the process with the remaining vegetables.

◆ Transfer the vegetables to a warm bowl and sprinkle the cayenne pepper, paprika, salt and pepper to taste over them. Toss lightly and serve.

EACH SERVING CONTAINS
Kcals 400 • Protein 14g • Fat 25g (of which saturated 3g) • Carbohydrate 29g
Fibre 7g • Kcals from fat 50% • Good source of vitamin C and folic acid

Parsley and Garlic Pitta Toasts

These are a lighter version of garlic bread. I can guarantee that everyone you serve them to will love them. As with many of the other starters, they can be served with a soup or salad to make a lunch dish.

Serves 4
Preparation time: 10 minutes
Cooking time: 10 minutes

4 large pitta breads

3 tablespoons extra virgin olive
  oil

3 garlic cloves, crushed

handful of fresh flat-leaf parsley,
  roughly chopped, to serve

◆ Preheat the oven to 180°C/350°F/Gas 4. Slice each pitta bread in half lengthways, then cut each half into 4–5 strips. Put in a single layer on a baking tray and bake for 10 minutes until golden and crispy.

◆ Heat the oil in a frying pan. Add the garlic and fry gently for a few minutes until softened. Drizzle the garlicky oil over the pitta slices and scatter the parsley over them.

Spicy pitta toasts
These don't use any kind of herb, and rely on spices for their flavour. Follow the recipe above, but replace the garlic with ½ teaspoon cayenne pepper and 1 teaspoon paprika.

Crunchy Marmite toasts
For 4 servings, turn the grill to high and toast 4 thick slices of white bread on one side only. Spread the untoasted sides with Marmite and scatter sesame seeds over them (1 tablespoon for each slice). Push the seeds into the bread slices, then put the toasts back under the grill, seeded sides upwards, and toast them until they are golden at the edges. Cut each slice into 4 squares and serve warm. These toasts go particularly well with Tomato Soup with Coriander Salsa (see page 48).

EACH SERVING CONTAINS
Parsley and Garlic Pitta Toasts and Spicy Pitta Toasts – Kcals 300 • Protein 7g • Fat 12g (of which
saturated 2g) • Carbohydrate 43g • Fibre 1.5g • Kcals from fat 36%
Crunchy Marmite Toasts – Kcals 185 • Protein 6.5g • Fat 9g (of which saturated 1.5g)
Carbohydrate 20g • Fibre 2g • Kcals from fat 46%

Puréed Chick Peas with Griddled Vegetables

One cup of cooked chick peas provides a quarter of an adult's daily protein requirement, one and a half times the folic acid requirement, half the iron and a fifth of the zinc. This purée also makes a great dip served with strips of toasted pitta bread or potato crisps.

Serves 4
Preparation time: 10 minutes
Cooking time: 10 minutes

415g (14½oz) can chick peas

1 garlic clove, roughly chopped

juice of ½ lime

3 tablespoons extra virgin olive oil

handful of freshly chopped flat-leaf
   parsley

olive oil, for brushing

115g (4oz) asparagus

115g (4oz) baby corn

115g (4oz) baby carrots

Maldon salt and freshly ground
   black pepper

◆ Drain the chick peas and reserve half their liquid. Put the chick peas and reserved liquid, garlic, lime juice and oil in a food processor and process to a smooth purée. Season with salt and pepper and mix in the freshly chopped parsley.

◆ Brush a griddle pan or heavy-based frying pan with a little oil and heat until it is very hot. Add the vegetables and cook them, turning frequently, for 5 minutes or until golden and cooked.

◆ Serve the vegetables warm with the soft, creamy purée as an accompaniment.

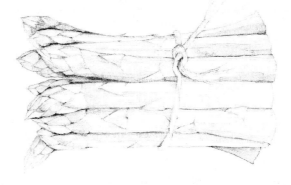

EACH SERVING CONTAINS
Kcals 285 • Protein 10g • Fat 17g (of which saturated 2g) • Carbohydrate 24g
Fibre 6g • Kcals from fat 55% • Good source of vitamin A

Warm Butter Bean Purée

It makes a welcome change to serve a warm rather than chilled dip and this purée is always a big hit. Serve it with fingers of hot toast or sea salt kettle chips. It also goes well with polenta, griddled vegetables or mashed potato. The cayenne pepper adds quite a kick, so if you feel the dip needs a sprinkling of colour before serving, it is advisable to dust a little paprika, rather than extra cayenne, over the top.

Serves 4
Preparation time: 15 minutes
Cooking time: 20 minutes

415g (14½oz) can butter beans, drained
1 large potato, about 225g (8oz), peeled and cut into chunks
1 bay leaf
4 tablespoons olive oil
1 medium-sized onion, chopped
1 tablespoon cayenne pepper
3 garlic cloves, crushed

1 tablespoon lemon juice
Maldon salt and freshly ground black pepper

To serve
pinch of cayenne pepper (optional)
handful fresh coriander leaves, roughly chopped

◆ Mash the beans into a coarse purée and set aside.

◆ Bring a small saucepan of water to the boil, add the potato chunks and bay leaf, and simmer for 10–15 minutes until the potato is tender. Drain, discard the bay leaf, and return the saucepan to the heat. Dry the potato over a very low heat, shaking the pan gently, then mash it.

◆ While the potato is boiling, heat 1 tablespoon oil in a frying pan and fry the onion, cayenne pepper and 2 garlic cloves for about 10 minutes or until the onion is soft. Add the puréed beans and mashed potato to the onion and mix well. Warm the mixture through over a low heat, stirring every now and then to make sure the purée doesn't stick to the pan.

◆ Beat the remaining crushed garlic and olive oil into the purée, add the coriander and season to taste with salt, pepper and the lemon juice. Dust with a sprinkling of cayenne pepper, if using, and serve warm.

EACH SERVING CONTAINS
Kcals 230 • Protein 7g • Fat 12g (of which saturated 1.5g)
Carbohydrate 25g • Fibre 6g • Kcals from fat 46%

Baked Asparagus with Garlic Croutons

It is not surprising to learn that asparagus has been the pride of the vegetable garden since the Renaissance – every way I cook it, I love it. This recipe looks stylish, is simple to make and is a wonderful starter, especially when the asparagus is served with fresh little garlic croutons. Avoid large tasteless spears and go for young ones that are full of flavour. Fresh spears are firm with tightly closed scales on the tips.

Serves 6
Preparation time: 15 minutes
Cooking time: 20 minutes

450g (1lb) fresh asparagus
2 tablespoons olive oil
6 field mushrooms, about 225g
   (8oz) total
freshly ground black pepper
handful of fresh flat-leaf parsley
   leaves, to serve

For the croutons
3 slices white bread, about 2.5cm
   (1in) thick
2 garlic cloves, crushed
4 tablespoons extra virgin olive oil

◆ Preheat the oven to 200°C/400°F/Gas 6. Break the tough ends off the asparagus (they should snap quite easily).

◆ Bring a saucepan of water to the boil, add the asparagus spears and simmer for 3–4 minutes. They must be firm and not tender. Drain the spears well on kitchen paper for a few minutes then transfer them to a shallow ovenproof dish.

◆ Heat the olive oil in a frying pan and sauté the mushrooms for 5–6 minutes until they are brown and soft. Slice each mushroom diagonally and place the slices on top of the asparagus. Drizzle the pan juices over the asparagus and mushrooms.

◆ Make the croutons: Cut the slices of bread into 2.5cm (1in) squares and place these on a baking tray in a single layer. Mix the garlic and oil together in a bowl and drizzle the mixture over the bread cubes. Bake in the oven for 10 minutes or until golden, turning the croutons once.

◆ Divide the baked asparagus between 6 warm serving plates, scatter the croutons, pepper and a few parsley leaves over them and serve immediately.

EACH SERVING CONTAINS
Kcals 250 • Protein 7g • Fat 12g (of which saturated 2g) • Carbohydrate 28g
Fibre 2.5g • Kcals from fat 45%

Hot Griddled Sweet Potato with Watercress Salsa

Watercress is a favourite ingredient of mine because of its peppery flavour and crunchy texture. Also, each leaf is packed with vitamins and minerals. I think it is underused and underrated in our cooking today – rocket seems to appear far more often on restaurant menus. Watercress adds colour, texture and a spicy kick to this crispy salsa, as it does to other cold dishes. It is also great in hot dishes, especially stir-fries. Add it just before the end of cooking so that the pretty green leaves have only enough time to wilt.

Serves 4
Preparation time: 15 minutes
Cooking time: 30 minutes

6 ripe plum tomatoes

½ cucumber, unpeeled

big bunch of watercress, roughly
   chopped

3 tablespoons olive oil

juice of ½ lime

½ red chilli, seeded and chopped

4 medium-sized sweet potatoes,
   unpeeled

olive oil, for brushing

Maldon salt and freshly ground
   black pepper

◆ Put the tomatoes in a bowl and cover with boiling water. Leave them for exactly 20 seconds then plunge them straight into cold water. Drain, skin and chop the tomatoes.

◆ Cut the cucumber in half lengthways, scoop out the seeds with a teaspoon and dice the flesh. Mix the cucumber with the tomatoes and watercress and transfer to a serving bowl.

◆ Put the 3 tablespoons olive oil and the lime juice and chilli into a screw-top jar and shake well to blend the ingredients. Drizzle the dressing over the salsa. Cover the bowl with cling film and chill until needed.

◆ Gently scrub the potatoes to clean them. Bring a large saucepan of water to the boil, add the potatoes and simmer for about 20 minutes until tender. To test, stick the point of a sharp knife into a potato – it should just go through the middle. Drain and leave to cool.

◆ Cut the potatoes into 2.5cm (1in) slices. Brush a little olive oil on both sides of each slice, and sprinkle with salt and pepper. Heat a griddle pan or heavy-based frying pan until hot and cook the potato slices for 2 minutes on each side until golden brown.

◆ Divide the potatoes between 4 warm bowls, top with the crispy watercress salsa and serve.

EACH SERVING CONTAINS
Kcals 330 • Protein 5g • Fat 15g (of which saturated 2.4g) • Carbohydrate 47g • Fibre 7g
Kcals from fat 41% • Excellent source of vitamins C, A, E • Good source of iron

Beetroot with Vinaigrette

Raw beetroot is packed with vitamin C – most of which is lost, along with its wonderful colour, when the vegetable is boiled. I hope this recipe will help you to enjoy this root in its raw and attractive state. I have added a little fresh apple – my first choice is always the little sweet Cox. Beetroot has a wonderful affinity with this fruit, which accentuates its natural sweetness and provides a little, much needed, acidity. I have also added some walnuts, and walnut oil, which both complement, and contrast with, the beetroot's flavour and texture. Use an extra 1 tablespoon olive oil if you do not have walnut oil.

Serves 4
Preparation time: 15 minutes
Cooking time: 2–3 minutes

pinch of Maldon salt	3 tablespoons olive oil
pinch of freshly ground black pepper	1 tablespoon walnut oil
½ teaspoon Dijon mustard	2 large raw beetroot
2–4 tablespoons white wine vinegar, depending on how tart you like your vinaigrette	3 sweet eating apples
	50g (1¾oz) walnuts
	75g (2½oz) fresh rocket
	large handful of watercress

◆ Mix the salt, pepper and mustard into the vinegar. Stir until the salt has dissolved, then gradually whisk in the olive and walnut oils with a fork.

◆ Peel the beetroot, cut each one into large chunks and grate them. Peel, core and grate the apples. Combine the beetroot and apples, add the vinaigrette and mix well. Set aside.

◆ Dry-fry the walnuts in a heavy-based frying pan, turning or stirring frequently, until golden. Allow the nuts to cool a little, then chop them roughly.

◆ Divide the rocket and watercress between 4 serving plates and spoon the beetroot on top. Scatter the walnuts over the beetroot and serve.

EACH SERVING CONTAINS
Kcals195 • Protein 2g • Fat 19g (of which saturated 2g) • Carbohydrate 3g
Fibre 1g • Kcals from fat 90% • Good source of vitamin C

Rich Mushrooms on Toast with Truffle Oil

I can almost predict that whenever I go to a restaurant in autumn I will order a vegetarian dish that has more than its fair share of wild mushrooms. There is something quite magical about chanterelles and porcini – they add a wonderfully intense flavour to other ingredients. Although the price for these delicacies may be high, the consolation is that you only need a few to have a really dramatic impact on a finished dish. I have chosen to use dried porcini in this recipe but morels are just as good. Drizzle the truffle oil – or a little extra virgin olive oil if this is too expensive – around each plate to finish the dish. Remember, you eat with your eyes!

Serves 4
Preparation time: 15 minutes, plus 20 minutes standing time
Cooking time: 15 minutes

30g (1oz) dried porcini

300ml (10fl oz) boiling water

250g (9oz) field mushrooms

150g (5½oz) closed-cap
  mushrooms

30g (1oz) butter

1 tablespoon extra virgin olive oil

2 garlic cloves, sliced

4 slices fresh white bread

To serve

handful of fresh flat-leaf parsley,
  chopped

2 teaspoons truffle oil

◆ Cover the porcini with the boiling water and leave to soak for 30 minutes. Drain and roughly chop the porcini.

◆ Cut the field and closed-cap mushrooms into thick slices. Heat the butter and oil in a frying pan, add the garlic and fry, stirring frequently, for 1 minute over a low heat without browning. Add the sliced field and closed-cap mushrooms and fry, stirring, for 1 minute. Add the chopped porcini and fry for a further10 minutes, stirring now and then.

◆ While the mushrooms are cooking, toast the slices of bread.

◆ Put a slice of toast on each of 4 warm plates and divide the mushrooms between them. Scatter chopped parsley over the mushrooms, drizzle a little truffle oil around each plate and serve immediately.

EACH SERVING CONTAINS
Kcals 200 • Protein 7g • Fat 11g (of which saturated 5g) • Carbohydrate 19g
Fibre 2.5g • Kcals from fat 51%

Mushrooms with Peppercorns and Garlic

Everyone loves garlic mushrooms and this recipe takes that familiar dish one step further. It is inspired by the spices I saw growing in Zanzibar. There are so many that I want to incorporate in my recipes and here I use lots of red and green peppercorns, which differ in colour and flavour simply because of the time when they were picked. Unlike some other cultivated mushrooms, shiitake have a very distinctive flavour and texture that can add a little excitement to other fresh cultivated mushrooms. This makes a delicious starter served with fresh bread rolls – or a main course when it is accompanied by a pile of steaming mashed potato. Use a mixture of black and white peppercorns if red and green ones are unavailable.

Serves 4
Preparation time: 10 minutes
Cooking time: 15 minutes

1 teaspoon mixed red and green peppercorns

125g (4½oz) shiitake mushrooms

125g (4½oz) chestnut mushrooms

125g (4½oz) field mushrooms

2 tablespoons olive oil

1 large onion, sliced

2 garlic cloves, crushed

150ml (5fl oz) vegetable stock

1–2 dashes of Tabasco sauce

handful of fresh coriander leaves, roughly chopped, to serve

◆ Dry-fry the peppercorns in a heavy-based frying pan over a moderate heat, turning or stirring frequently, for 2 minutes or until they start to pop. Coarsely crush the peppercorns using a pestle and mortar.

◆ Tear the shiitake mushrooms into strips. Slice the chestnut mushrooms into quarters and the field mushrooms into thin strips.

◆ Heat the oil in a frying pan and fry the onion over a moderate heat for 5 minutes or until softened. Add the garlic and crushed peppercorns and fry for a further 2 minutes. Add the mushrooms and fry for a further 5 minutes.

◆ Heat the stock until simmering and pour it over the mushrooms. Simmer the mixture for 2 minutes or until the stock has evaporated. Add Tabasco sauce to taste. Scatter fresh coriander leaves over the mushrooms and serve immediately.

EACH SERVING CONTAINS
Kcals 80 • Protein 3g • Fat 6g (of which saturated 0.85g) • Carbohydrate 3.5g
Fibre 1g • Kcals from fat 70%

Crunchy Baked Tomatoes with Lime, Onion and Chilli

It is important that the tomatoes have lots of flavour – all too often, the larger they are, the less flavour they have. If this is the case, use twelve smaller tomatoes bursting with flavour rather than eight large ones. Ever since I drizzled lime juice over tomatoes before roasting them I have found the combination hard to beat. This makes a lovely starter served with fresh bread or a wonderful main course accompanied by hot potatoes or polenta.

Serves 4
Preparation time: 10 minutes
Cooking time: 10 minutes

8 or 12 medium-sized vine-ripened tomatoes

2 bunches of spring onions, finely chopped

1 small red chilli, seeded and finely chopped

2.5cm (1in) piece fresh root ginger, peeled and finely chopped

2 garlic cloves, finely chopped

2 tablespoons fresh basil leaves, roughly torn

a 50g (1¾oz) packet plain potato crisps

juice of 1 lime

juice of 1 orange

2 tablespoons extra virgin olive oil

Maldon salt and freshly ground black pepper

◆ Preheat the grill to high. Slice off the tops of the tomatoes and scoop out the seeds and juice with a teaspoon. Turn the tomatoes upside down as you do so to allow them to drain slightly. Dry the insides of the tomatoes with kitchen paper and season with salt and pepper.

◆ Combine the spring onions, chilli, ginger, garlic and basil and mix well. Fill the tomatoes with this mixture and crumble a few crisps over the mixture. Drizzle the lime and orange juices and olive oil over the top of each tomato.

◆ Put under the grill for about 2 minutes until the tomatoes are warm and the onion mixture is just turning golden. Serve immediately.

EACH SERVING CONTAINS
Kcals 210 • Protein 3g • Fat 16g (of which saturated 3.5g) • Carbohydrate 14g • Fibre 3g
Kcals from fat 69% • Excellent source of vitamin C • Good source of vitamins A and E

Baby Mediterranean Tarts with Fresh Basil Purée

These tarts are a perfect example of how to combine ease with stylish presentation. Make sure you have plenty of fresh basil leaves to scatter over them just before serving. The Rustica crushed tomatoes are a key ingredient; unlike canned tomatoes they are picked and packed within 30 minutes and their flavour is simply stunning. The tarts can be prepared in advance, then covered with cling film until you are ready to bake them.

Serves 4
Preparation time: 15 minutes
Cooking time:15 minutes

3 garlic cloves, sliced

30 fresh basil leaves

3 tablespoons extra virgin olive oil

juice of 1 lemon

28 × 23cm (11 × 9in) sheet of
frozen ready-rolled puff pastry,
thawed

4 tablespoons Cirio Rustica
crushed tomatoes

10 pitted black olives, sliced

Maldon salt and freshly ground
black pepper

handful of fresh basil leaves,
roughly torn, to serve

♦ Preheat the oven to 225°C/425°F/Gas 7. Put the garlic and fresh basil in a food processor and process to a paste. Add the oil and lemon juice and process the mixture until blended. Alternatively, chop the garlic and fresh basil and mix thoroughly with the oil and lemon juice. Season to taste with salt and pepper.

♦ Use a round cutter or egg cup to cut out twenty 4cm (1½in) circles of pastry. Put the circles straight on to a baking sheet and prick them all over with a fork. Spoon a little of the crushed tomatoes on to each pastry circle, top with a few olive slices and season to taste with salt and pepper. Drizzle 1 teaspoon basil purée over each tart.

♦ Put the tarts in the oven and bake for 10–12 minutes until risen and golden. Divide them between 4 warm plates and drizzle 1 teaspoon basil purée over them. Scatter a few basil leaves on top and serve hot. For a really dramatic look, drizzle the remaining basil purée around each plate.

EACH SERVING CONTAINS
Kcals 290 • Protein 3g • Fat 22g (of which saturated 1g) • Carbohydrate 21g
Fibre 0.5g • Kcals from fat 68%

Fried Tomato Toasts

There is something quite delicious about hot fried bread topped with soft cool tomatoes, and the addition of fresh basil and black pepper takes it into a different world. Some people are lucky enough to enjoy picking fresh, sun-ripened tomatoes straight from the vine, when the red and round fruits are at their sweetest. For those of us who are not so fortunate, many types are available nowadays, so it is slightly easier to find a variety that has both flavour and texture. Choose one with a skin that is not too tough or thick and a flesh that is succulent.

Serves 4
Preparation time: 10 minutes
Cooking time: 10 minutes

---

8 ripe plum tomatoes

4 slices fresh herb bread *or* white
  bread

vegetable oil, for frying

large handful of fresh basil leaves

Maldon salt and freshly ground
  black pepper

extra virgin olive oil, to drizzle

◆ Put the tomatoes in a bowl and cover with boiling water. Leave them for exactly 20 seconds then plunge them straight into cold water. Drain, skin and roughly chop the tomatoes. Set aside.

◆ Cut each slice of bread into quarters. Heat a little vegetable oil in a large frying pan and fry the bread quarters until they are golden on both sides.

◆ Divide the bread quarters between 4 warm serving plates and top them with the tomatoes. Stack about 6 basil leaves together, roll them into a cigar shape and cut this into thin strips. Repeat with the remaining basil leaves. Scatter the strips of basil over the tomatoes and season well with salt and pepper. Drizzle a little extra virgin olive oil around each plate and serve.

EACH SERVING CONTAINS
Kcals 245 • Protein 4.5g • Fat 15g (of which saturated 2g) • Carbohydrate 23g
Fibre 2.5g • Kcals from fat 57% • Good source of vitamin C

Blood Oranges with Red Onions, Black Olives and Fennel Dressing

One average-sized orange will generally supply an adult's daily vitamin C requirement. If you can find blood oranges, you will not be disappointed – they look amazing and taste sweet and juicy. If they are not available, choose the juiciest possible large oranges.

Serves 4
Preparation time: 20 minutes

2 red onions, thinly sliced

150g (5½oz) black olives, pitted

4 blood oranges

For the fennel dressing
1 fennel bulb

juice of 1 lemon

3 tablespoons extra virgin olive oil

Maldon salt and freshly ground
black pepper

◆ Put the red onions and olives in a bowl.

◆ Peel the oranges, working around the fruit with a sharp knife. Then cut the segments of flesh away from the membrane with the knife. Put the flesh in the bowl with the red onions and olives. Repeat with the remaining oranges.

◆ Make the fennel dressing: Trim the tough stalks off the fennel bulb, shave off the base and remove any damaged outer layers. Slice the bulb in half lengthways, cut out the core and slice each half into thin strips. Combine the lemon juice and olive oil, season to taste with salt and pepper and mix with the fennel slices.

◆ Toss the orange segments, onions and olives lightly together. Drizzle the fennel dressing over them and serve.

EACH SERVING CONTAINS
Kcals 185 • Protein 3g • Fat 12g (of which saturated 2g) • Carbohydrate 17g
Fibre 5g • Kcals from fat 58% • Excellent source of vitamin C

Potatoes with Broad Beans and Mint Vinaigrette

Whenever you make potato salad add the dressing to the warm vegetables and leave them to cool. The juicy dressing will soak into the hot potatoes so that every bite oozes with flavour.

Serves 4
Preparation time: 10 minutes
Cooking time: about 15 minutes

900g (2lb) new potatoes, unpeeled

150g (5½oz) broad beans, shelled

For the mint vinaigrette
2 large handfuls of fresh mint
leaves

4 tablespoons extra virgin olive oil

juice of 1 lemon

1 tablespoon coarse-grain mustard

pinch of golden caster sugar

Maldon salt and freshly ground
black pepper

To serve
4 spring onions, thinly sliced
diagonally

handful of fresh mint leaves

♦ Put the potatoes in boiling water and simmer for about 15 minutes until almost cooked. They should be just tender when pierced with the point of a knife. Add the beans and simmer for a further 5 minutes until the potatoes are cooked and the beans are just tender. Drain and put in a serving dish.

♦ While the vegetables are cooking, make the mint vinaigrette: Put the mint and olive oil in a food processor or blender. Add the lemon juice, mustard and sugar and season to taste with salt and pepper. Process until blended.

♦ Drizzle the vinaigrette over the warm potatoes and beans, toss gently so that the vegetables are well coated and leave to cool. Scatter the spring onions and fresh mint leaves over the salad and serve.

EACH SERVING CONTAINS
Kcals 300 • Protein 7g • Fat 12g (of which saturated 1.5g) • Carbohydrate 42g
Fibre 5.5g • Kcals from fat 37% • Good source of vitamins B_1, B_6, folic acid, C

Avocado with Beans and Coriander

*I generally remove the skins from tomatoes unless the fruit is very ripe.
Crisp tortilla chips work really well as a contrast to the softness of the
avocado and tomatoes in this little starter.*

Serves 4
Preparation time: 15 minutes

200g (7oz) vine-ripened tomatoes

415g (14½oz) can cannellini beans,
   drained

200g (7oz) can sweetcorn, drained

1 red chilli, seeded and sliced

juice of ½ lime

1 avocado

100g (3½oz) plain corn tortilla chips

2 tablespoons extra virgin olive oil

handful of fresh coriander leaves,
   roughly chopped, to serve

◆ Put the tomatoes in a bowl and cover with boiling water. Leave them for
exactly 20 seconds then plunge them straight into cold water. Drain and
skin the tomatoes and remove their seeds with a teaspoon. Roughly chop
the flesh.

◆ Put the chopped tomato, beans, sweetcorn, chilli and lime juice in a large
bowl. Slice the avocado in half lengthways and remove the stone. Peel the
avocado, then chop the flesh into little chunks and add to the beans and
tomato.

◆ Arrange the tortilla chips in a single layer on a serving dish. Pile the
avocado mixture and beans on top and drizzle the olive oil over it. Scatter
the coriander leaves over the salad and serve.

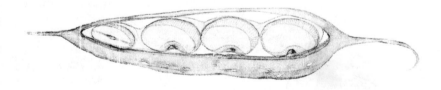

EACH SERVING CONTAINS
Kcals 410 • Protein 11g • Fat 20g (of which saturated 3.5g) • Carbohydrate 48g
Fibre 10g • Kcals from fat 44% • Good source of vitamins C and E

Roasted Apple, Onion and Sweet Potato Soup

Despite their name, sweet potatoes are not related to potatoes. However, they will do most things that potatoes do. They enjoy being roasted, baked or mashed and are a great thickener for soups. They have their own natural sweetness, which is why I have added a few tart apples to help balance the flavours. They seem to enjoy being mixed with flavours like ginger, chilli, lime and coriander as well as the fennel and cumin used here. You could always add a few parsnips to the roasting dish if they are in season – sweet potatoes work really well with other root vegetables.

Serves 4
Preparation time: 20 minutes
Cooking time: 50 minutes

1½ teaspoons fennel seeds

1 teaspoon cumin seeds

450g (1lb) baby onions, quartered

3 large sweet potatoes, peeled and roughly chopped

3 apples, preferably a tart variety such as Granny Smith

3 tablespoons olive oil

900ml (1½ pints) vegetable stock

Maldon salt and freshly ground black pepper

handful of fresh tarragon leaves, to serve

◆ Preheat the oven to 230°C/450°F/Gas 8. Dry-fry the fennel and cumin seeds in a heavy-based frying pan over a moderate heat, turning or stirring frequently, for 3 minutes or until they start to go brown and pop. Coarsely crush the seeds using a pestle and mortar.

◆ Put the onions and sweet potatoes into a roasting dish. Core and roughly chop 2 apples and add them to the dish. Sprinkle the crushed seeds over the vegetables and apples and season. Drizzle 2 tablespoons olive oil over the top. Roast for 25 minutes, then turn the vegetables over and roast for a further 25 minutes. The onions should be tender when pierced with a knife. Remove 2 potato chunks and 8 onion quarters and set them aside.

◆ Put half the remaining vegetables into a food processor with half the stock and process to a smooth purée. Transfer to a saucepan. Repeat with the remaining vegetables and stock. Warm the soup through over a gentle heat.

▶

- Core and roughly chop the reserved apple. Roughly chop the 2 reserved potato chunks and the 8 reserved onion quarters. Heat the remaining oil in a frying pan, add the chopped apple and sauté for 5 minutes or until golden. Add the chopped potatoes and onions and warm through, stirring every now and then, over a low heat.

- When the soup is warm, divide it between 4 warm bowls and spoon a little of the chopped onion, potato and apple mixture into the centre of each bowl. Scatter the fresh tarragon leaves over the soup and serve.

EACH SERVING CONTAINS
Kcals 340 • Protein 5g • Fat 9g (of which saturated 1.5g) • Carbohydrate 64g • Fibre 8g
Kcals from fat 25% • Excellent source of vitamins A and E • Good source of vitamins B₁ and C

Thai Pumpkin and Coconut Soup

I have eaten something similar to this soup in a variety of restaurants and it always tastes good. If pumpkins are not in season, use the same quantity of sweet potatoes – they love lively ingredients like chillis, soy sauce and coconut milk. Coconut cream is one of those magical ingredients that can add a really intense creaminess to many dishes.

Serves 4
Preparation time: 15 minutes
Cooking time: 40 minutes

170g (6oz) rice noodles

675g (1½lb) pumpkin, peeled and cut into bite-sized chunks

4 tablespoons olive oil

½ teaspoon dried chilli flakes

400g (14oz) can unsweetened coconut milk

75g (2½oz) coconut cream

450ml (15fl oz) vegetable stock (see page 55)

2 tablespoons light soy sauce

2 teaspoons soft brown sugar

75g (2½oz) bean sprouts

75g (2½oz) carrots, cut into thin strips

Maldon salt and freshly ground black pepper

large handful of fresh coriander leaves, roughly chopped, to serve

◆ Preheat the oven to 220°C/425°F/Gas 7. Prepare the rice noodles according to the packet instructions. Put the pumpkin into a roasting dish, drizzle 2 tablespoons olive oil over it and season. Roast for 40 minutes or until tender.

◆ While the pumpkin is roasting, heat the remaining oil in a frying pan. Add the chilli flakes and sauté them over a moderate heat for about 2 minutes. Add the coconut milk, coconut cream and vegetable stock and simmer gently, stirring, until the cream has dissolved. Stir in the soy sauce and sugar. Season well. Mix in the bean sprouts and carrots and simmer for a further 1 minute. Add the rice noodles and warm them through.

◆ Divide the chunks of pumpkin between 4 warm serving bowls and pour the soup over them. Scatter lots of fresh coriander over the top and serve.

EACH SERVING CONTAINS
Kcals 445 • Protein 5g • Fat 26g (of which saturated 14g) • Carbohydrate 44g
Fibre 2.5g • Kcals from fat 52% • Good source of vitamins C and A

Tomato Soup with Coriander Salsa

I often turn this into a sorbet and serve it as a starter or between courses. Remember always to skin the tomatoes, or you will end up with tough bits of skin in an otherwise smooth soup.

Serves 4
Preparation time: 20 minutes
Cooking time: 20 minutes

900g (2lb) ripe tomatoes

1 tablespoon olive oil

1 large onion, finely sliced

2 garlic cloves, crushed

1 teaspoon lime juice

pinch of soft brown sugar

handful of fresh coriander leaves

zest of 1 lime

**Maldon salt and freshly ground
 black pepper**

◆ Skin the tomatoes (see page 41) and dice the flesh.

◆ Heat the oil in a large saucepan and fry the onion and garlic over a low heat, stirring, for 10 minutes until the onion is cooked but not brown. Reserve 2 tablespoons of the tomato flesh and add the remainder to the saucepan. Cook gently for 10 minutes. Add the lime juice, 400ml (14fl oz) water and the sugar. Bring to the boil then reduce the heat and simmer for 5 minutes. Leave to cool slightly.

◆ Put the soup in a food processor and process to a smooth purée. Pass the purée through a sieve into a clean saucepan and season to taste. Add half the coriander leaves and warm the soup through over a gentle heat.

◆ Divide the soup between 4 warm serving bowls. Mix the reserved diced tomato, remaining coriander leaves and the lime zest together and put a spoonful of the salsa in the middle of each bowl. Serve.

For a tomato sorbet
Leave the purée until it is cold, then add a couple of dashes of Tabasco sauce. Either process the purée in an ice-cream machine, following the manufacturer's instructions, or pour it into a freezeproof container and freeze it for 3 hours. Take it out of the freezer every hour, mash it with a fork and return it to the freezer. Serve with a little drizzle of vodka over the top of each serving and sticks of celery, or with the coriander salsa.

EACH SERVING CONTAINS
Kcals 75 • Protein 2g • Fat 3g (of which saturated 0.6g) • Carbohydrate 10g
Fibre 3g • Kcals from fat 42% • Good source of vitamins C and A

Corn, Coconut, Lime and Basil Soup

I try to make soups with ingredients that provide the flavour rather than having to rely heavily on stocks. The stock for this particular recipe is made from the corn cobs left over when the kernels have been removed. However, if fresh corn is not in season, use a 400g (14oz) can of sweetcorn and a good vegetable stock (see page 55) instead. Similarly, if kaffir lime leaves, which add a wonderfully subtle citrus flavour to the soup, are not available, substitute the fine zest (no pith) of half a lime. (There are always ways around these little challenges.) Jalapeño chillies are probably the best-known chillies around. They are about 2.5–4cm (1–1½in) long with a full flavour and medium heat. As with most chillies the heat is concentrated in the seeds and the membrane which holds the seeds to the flesh.

Serves 4
Preparation time: 20 minutes
Cooking time: 15 minutes, plus 1¼ hours for boiling the stock, if making

---

4 cobs of corn

2 tablespoons vegetable oil

2.5cm (1in) piece fresh root ginger, peeled and grated

2 shallots, sliced

1 jalapeño chilli, seeded and finely chopped

3 kaffir lime leaves *or* zest of ½ lime

120ml (4fl oz) unsweetened coconut milk

large handful of fresh basil leaves

2 limes, each cut into chunks, to serve

◆ Scrape the kernels from the cobs with a sharp knife and put the kernels in a bowl. Set aside.

◆ Break each of the cobs into 2 or 3 pieces, put them in a large saucepan and add 1.5 litres (2¾ pints) water. Bring to the boil then reduce the heat and simmer, covered, for 1 hour. You will need to skim the foam from the top of the liquid with a large spoon, especially for the first 30 minutes. Strain the stock through a fine-mesh strainer or cheesecloth.

◆ Heat the oil in a large clean saucepan and add the ginger, shallots and chilli. Fry gently for 5 minutes, stirring frequently, until the shallots are softened. Add the kaffir lime leaves or lime zest, reserved corn stock (or the equivalent volume of vegetable stock) and coconut milk. Bring up to the boil, then reduce heat immediately and simmer for 5 minutes. Add water, if

▶

necessary, to achieve the texture you prefer. Add the reserved kernels and simmer for another 5 minutes.

◆ Ladle the soup into warm bowls. Stack about 6 basil leaves together, roll them into a cigar shape and slice thinly. Repeat with the remaining basil. Scatter the basil strips over the soup. Serve with wedges of lime.

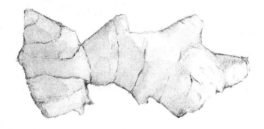

EACH SERVING CONTAINS
Kcals 210 • Protein 5g • Fat 11g (of which saturated 3.6g) • Carbohydrate 23g
Fibre 2.6g • Kcals from fat 48%

Creamy Carrot and Ginger Soup with Curly Toasts

For most of us soup means breaking bread and sharing, which may be why I always tend to make soup if there are friends or family for lunch or supper. This soup is rich and tasty without using lots of fat. I want everyone to feel good about eating it and asking for seconds without feeling guilty.

Serves 4
Preparation time: 15 minutes
Cooking time: 35 minutes

---

4 teaspoons cumin seeds

2.25kg (5lb) carrots, diced

2.5cm (1in) piece fresh root ginger, peeled and sliced

4 slices of day-old soft grain bread

Maldon salt and freshly ground black pepper

handful of fresh coriander leaves, roughly chopped, to serve

◆ Preheat the oven to 180°C/350°F/Gas 4. Dry-fry the cumin seeds in a heavy-based frying pan over a moderate heat, turning or stirring frequently, for 5 minutes or until golden. Coarsely crush the seeds using a pestle and mortar. Put the carrots, ginger and half the cumin in a large saucepan and pour in enough water to just cover the carrots. Simmer, covered, for 30 minutes or until the carrots are soft.

◆ While the carrots are cooking, toast the slices of bread lightly on both sides. Cut off the crusts and cut each slice in half horizontally. Carefully scrape off any doughy bits, then cut each half slice into 2 squares and then 4 triangles. Arrange the triangles on a baking tray and bake for 10 minutes until golden and curly. Set aside.

◆ Drain the carrots over a bowl and reserve the cooking liquid. Put the carrots and 100ml (3½fl oz) of the reserved liquid in a food processor and process to a smooth purée. If the soup is too thick, add more cooking liquid.

◆ Rinse out the saucepan, return the soup and warm it through over a gentle heat. Season with salt, pepper and as much of the remaining cumin as you wish. Divide the soup between 4 coffee cups, scatter the fresh coriander over the top and pop the curly toasts on the saucers to serve.

EACH SERVING CONTAINS
Kcals 250 • Protein 7g • Fat 3g (of which saturated 0.5g) • Carbohydrate 48g • Fibre 14g
Kcals from fat 13% • Excellent source of vitamin A • Good source of vitamins E and C, folic acid

Roasted Squash Soup with Fresh Coriander

This is a soup for winter when butternut squash are easily available in markets and supermarkets. It is quick to prepare – the only time-consuming part is roasting the squash, but at least you can put them in the oven and do something else while they merrily cook away. Squash have a chameleon quality and are just as at home in a sweet tart (see Pecan and Butternut Squash Tart, page 175) as they are in a soup. Although the addition of vanilla is optional, I find it just rounds all the flavours off perfectly.

Serves 4
Preparation time: 15 minutes
Cooking time: 1½ hours

---

1 large butternut squash, about 900g (2 lb)

4 tablespoons olive oil

2 shallots, sliced

pinch of grated fresh nutmeg

1 cinnamon stick

big pinch of saffron threads

2 drops of vanilla extract (optional)

Maldon salt and freshly ground black pepper

large handful of fresh coriander leaves, roughly chopped

◆ Preheat the oven to 200°C/400°F/Gas 6. Rub the squash with 2 tablespoons oil then put it in a shallow roasting tin and bake for 1 hour. Leave to cool slightly.

◆ Slice the squash in half, scoop out the seeds with a teaspoon and remove the peel. Put the pulp into a bowl and mash it well.

◆ Heat the remaining oil in a large saucepan, add the shallots, nutmeg, cinnamon and saffron and fry over a moderate heat, stirring, for 5 minutes until the shallots are softened. Add the squash and sauté, stirring, for 2 minutes. Pour 600ml (1 pint) water into the saucepan, bring to the boil then reduce the heat. Add the vanilla extract, if using, and season with salt and pepper. Cover and simmer for 30 minutes – add more water, if necessary, to achieve the texture you prefer.

◆ Put the soup in a food processor and process to a smooth purée. Divide the soup among 4 warm bowls, scatter fresh coriander over the top and serve.

EACH SERVING CONTAINS
Kcals 185 • Protein 2.5g • Fat 11g (of which saturated 1.5g) • Carbohydrate 19.5g • Fibre 3.5g
Kcals from fat 55% • Excellent source of vitamins C and A • Good source of vitamin E

Wild Mushroom Soup

I tend not to use a lot of tofu in my vegan cooking, but this soup is perfect for it. The flavours from the mushrooms and harissa soak into the cubes of bean curd, adding texture and flavour to the finished dish. You can replace the vegetable stock with the same quantity of stock made with Swiss vegetable vegan bouillon powder. If you can find toasted sesame oil, use it instead of the plain version when you serve the soup.

Serves 4
Preparation time: 15 minutes
Cooking time: 10 minutes

225g (8oz) fresh oyster mushrooms
150g (5½oz) shiitake mushrooms
2 tablespoons vegetable oil
2 garlic cloves, crushed
5cm (2in) piece fresh root ginger,
  peeled and grated
200g (7oz) can straw mushrooms,
  drained
2 tablespoons sake
900ml (1½ pints) vegetable stock
  (see page 55)

2 tablespoons cornflour
125g (4½oz) firm tofu, diced
Maldon salt and freshly ground
  black pepper

To serve
2 teaspoons sesame oil
3 tablespoons sesame seeds

◆ Remove and discard the stalks of the oyster and shiitake mushrooms. Slice each mushroom in half.

◆ Heat the oil in a large saucepan. Add the garlic, ginger, sliced mushrooms and straw mushrooms and sauté over a moderate heat for 5 minutes or until the garlic and ginger are softened. Add the sake and stock and bring to the boil. Reduce the heat to a simmer.

◆ In a small bowl, mix the cornflour with 2 tablespoons warm water to form a smooth paste. Stir the paste into the soup. Continue stirring – the soup will thicken quite quickly. When the soup has thickened, add the tofu and season to taste with salt and pepper.

◆ Divide the soup between 4 warm bowls, drizzle a little sesame oil over each serving, scatter a few sesame seeds on top and serve.

EACH SERVING CONTAINS
Kcals 205 • Protein 8g • Fat 15g (of which saturated 2g) • Carbohydrate 8g
Fibre 2g • Kcals from fat 69%

Spicy Gazpacho Soup with Paprika Croutons

Traditional gazpacho is served cold. This warm version is delicious, topped with hot paprika croutons. Serve a little bowl of the croutons with the soup. If you are short of time, make the gazpacho – which is incredibly quick – and serve it with fresh bread.

Serves 4
Preparation time: 20 minutes
Cooking time: 30 minutes

900g (2lb) very ripe cherry
    tomatoes *or* baby plum
    tomatoes
1 cucumber, peeled and seeded
1 garlic clove, chopped
1 red chilli, seeded and finely
    chopped
3 spring onions, finely chopped
4 tablespoons extra virgin olive oil
1 tablespoon red wine vinegar
2 teaspoons golden caster sugar
15g (½oz) fresh wild rocket
pinch of cayenne pepper
Maldon salt

For the croutons
4 slices of white bread or ciabatta,
    about 2.5cm (1in) thick
4–5 tablespoons extra virgin olive
    oil
large pinch of Maldon salt
large pinch of paprika

To serve
pinch of cayenne pepper
handful of roughly torn fresh wild
    rocket leaves

◆ Preheat the oven to 190°C/375°F/Gas 5. Cut the bread into 2.5cm (1in) cubes and put in a bowl. Add the olive oil, salt and paprika and toss to coat the cubes. Place the cubes on a baking tray in a single layer and bake in the oven for about 20 minutes, turning once, until the croutons are golden and crispy on the outside but still moist in the middle.

◆ Put all the soup ingredients except the salt and cayenne pepper into a food processor and process to a smooth purée. Pour the soup into a saucepan and heat gently for 5–10 minutes or until warm, then season to taste.

◆ Divide the soup between 4 warm bowls. Top with a few croutons, sprinkle over a little cayenne and scatter torn rocket leaves over each serving. Serve immediately, with the remaining croutons in a small bowl.

EACH SERVING CONTAINS
Kcals 340 • Protein 5g • Fat 23g (of which saturated 3g) • Carbohydrate 29g • Fibre 3.5g
Kcals from fat 62% • Excellent source of vitamin C • Good source of vitamins A and E

Vegetable Stock

If you want to make stock for soups, this is for you. As with all recipes, the finished product will only be as good as its raw ingredients, so don't be tempted to use old vegetables that lack flavour. Freeze any stock you don't use immediately.

Makes 2.6 litres (4½ pints)
Preparation time: 20 minutes
Cooking time: 1¼ hours

2 tablespoons olive oil
3 medium-sized onions, roughly
   chopped
4 carrots, roughly chopped
2 leeks, roughly chopped
1 celery stick, roughly chopped
1 small green lettuce

½ head of broccoli, cut into florets
1 bay leaf
4 black peppercorns
pinch of Maldon salt
handful of fresh flat-leaf parsley,
   roughly chopped

◆ Heat the olive oil in a large saucepan. Add the onions, carrots, leeks, celery, lettuce and broccoli and sweat the vegetables over a low heat for 20 minutes. Add the bay leaf, peppercorns, salt, parsley and 3.4 litres (6 pints) water. Bring to the boil then reduce the heat and simmer, partially covered, for 1¼ hours over a very low heat – it is important that the liquid only just bubbles. Every now and then you will need to skim the foam from the top of the liquid with a large spoon.

◆ Strain the stock, making sure you don't push any of the vegetables through the sieve.

◆ Leave to cool and refrigerate (or freeze) until needed.

EACH SERVING CONTAINS
No significant nutrients

snacks & light meals

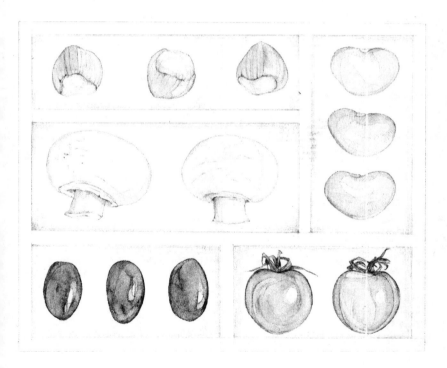

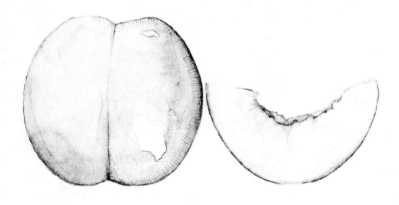

Moroccan Spiced Couscous with Fruits

I have a real passion for couscous, one of the truly great dishes of Morocco, Tunisia and Algeria. Couscous is made from strong or hard wheat, which is moistened with water and coated with a fine flour, then rolled into tiny cream-coloured pellets. Like other carbohydrates, couscous relies on the ingredients that you add to it for flavour and contrasting texture.

Serves 4
Preparation time: 15 minutes, plus standing time
Cooking time: 20 minutes

450g (1lb) couscous

250ml (8½fl oz) vegetable stock

pinch of saffron threads

55g (2oz) dried apricots, roughly chopped

55g (2oz) dates, stoned and roughly chopped

55g (2oz) raisins

pinch of chilli powder, preferably Kashmiri chilli powder

2 tablespoons lemon oil or olive oil

juice of 1 lemon

415g (14½oz) can chick peas, drained and rinsed

handful of fresh mint leaves, roughly chopped

handful of fresh coriander leaves, roughly chopped

75g (2½oz) flaked almonds

Maldon salt and freshly ground black pepper

◆ Preheat the oven to 200°C/400°F/Gas 6. Put the couscous in an ovenproof dish. Mix the stock, saffron, apricots, dates and raisins in a saucepan and bring to the boil. Pour the hot stock and fruit over the couscous. Add just enough boiling water to cover the grains, but do not flood them. Set aside for 15 minutes.

◆ Fluff up the couscous with a fork and season it with salt, pepper and chilli powder to taste. Drizzle the lemon or olive oil and lemon juice over and add the chick peas. Mix the ingredients well, then cover the dish.

◆ Bake the couscous for 15 minutes. Fluff up the grains, stir in the mint and coriander, and return the couscous to the oven for a further 5 minutes. Meanwhile, dry-fry the almonds in a heavy-based frying pan over a moderate heat, turning or stirring frequently, for 5 minutes until they are golden. Scatter the almonds over the couscous and serve immediately.

EACH SERVING CONTAINS
Kcals 630 • Protein 20g • Fat 20g (of which saturated 2g) • Carbohydrate 98g • Fibre 7g
Kcals from fat 29% • Excellent source of vitamins B_1, niacin, B_6 and E, also iron

Griddled Red Onion Slices with Couscous

Red onions cook really well on a griddle – they go soft in the middle and charred on the edges. If you have slightly more time, parboil the onions before griddling them. The texture and flavour will be slightly different, and equally as delicious. Leave the couscous to stand, covered, in a warm place for as long as possible after pouring warm water or vegetable stock (see page 55) over it. It will be much lighter and fluffier as a result. There are many ways of preparing couscous, but this one is my favourite.

Serves 4
Preparation time: 10 minutes, plus 30 minutes standing time
Cooking time: about 20 minutes

450g (1lb) couscous

4 red onions

olive oil, for griddling

juice of ½ lime

**Maldon salt and freshly ground
   black pepper**

To serve

**large handful of fresh flat-leaf
   parsley, roughly chopped**

1 lime, cut into 4 wedges

◆ Put the couscous in a bowl and add just enough warm water or vegetable stock to cover the grains, but do not flood them. Cover and leave for at least 30 minutes in a warm place.

◆ Cut the onions vertically into 1cm (½in) slices. Brush a griddle pan with a little olive oil and heat until very hot. Cook the onion slices for about 3–4 minutes on each side – you may need to do this in 2 batches. If you do not have a griddle pan, heat a grill until it is really hot and grill the onions for the same amount of time.

◆ Fluff up the grains of couscous with a fork, squeeze the lime juice over them and season well with salt and pepper. Divide the couscous between 4 warm plates. Arrange the onion slices on top of the couscous and scatter fresh parsley over the top. Serve with the lime wedges.

EACH SERVING CONTAINS
Kcals 310 • Protein 7.5g • Fat 4g (of which saturated 0.4g) • Carbohydrate 65g • Fibre 1g
Kcals from fat 12% • Good source of iron

Warm Couscous with Garlic, Black Olives and Tomatoes

I adore the combination of garlic, olives and tomatoes – it whisks me off to a Mediterranean country every time I eat it. The good news is that ten large olives contain about one-fifth of an adult's daily requirement of iron.

Serves 4

Preparation time: 15 minutes, plus 30 minutes standing time
Cooking time: 5 minutes

3 tablespoons extra virgin olive oil

1 garlic clove, crushed

450g (1lb) couscous

8 medium-sized vine-ripened plum
    tomatoes; choose juicy, ripe
    ones

200g (7oz) black olives, pitted

juice of ½ lemon

handful of fresh flat-leaf parsley,
    roughly chopped

Maldon salt and freshly ground
    black pepper

◆ Heat the olive oil in a saucepan, add the garlic and fry gently for 5 minutes or until it is softened but not brown. Add the couscous and stir until well coated. Remove the saucepan from the heat, and add just enough warm water to cover the grains, but do not flood them. Cover and leave for at least 30 minutes in a warm place.

◆ Put the tomatoes in a bowl and cover with boiling water. Leave them for exactly 20 seconds then plunge them straight into cold water. Drain and skin the tomatoes, then dice their flesh. Roughly chop the olives.

◆ Fluff up the grains of couscous with a fork and squeeze the lemon juice over them. Add the tomatoes and olives and half the parsley. Mix together. Season with salt and pepper. Divide between 4 warm plates, scatter the remaining parsley over the top and serve.

EACH SERVING CONTAINS
Kcals 380 • Protein 8g • Fat 12g (of which saturated 2g) • Carbohydrate 62g • Fibre 3g
Kcals from fat 30% • Excellent source of vitamin C • Good source of iron, vitamin E

Bright Red Pepper Pesto Linguine

The colour and flavour of this sauce is brilliant and intense. I developed the recipe while roasting peppers for a soup. There were some left over so I whizzed them in a food processor with a few other ingredients. Always wash your hands immediately after preparing fresh chillies, and be careful not to rub your eyes – you'll be in agony.

Serves 4
Preparation time: 20 minutes
Cooking time: 10–12 minutes

4 red peppers

2 red chillies

75g (2½oz) hazelnuts

large handful of fresh basil leaves

2 garlic cloves, crushed

3 tablespoons extra virgin olive oil,
   plus extra for tossing

340g (12oz) linguine

Maldon salt and freshly ground
   black pepper

handful of fresh basil leaves,
   roughly torn, to serve

◆ Preheat the grill to high. Put the peppers and chillies skin side up under the grill and cook until they are black and charred all over. Put them straight into a plastic bag. Seal and leave for 5 minutes – the steam will help to loosen the pepper and chilli skins.

◆ Peel the peppers and chillies and remove their seeds with a teaspoon. Dry-fry the hazelnuts in a heavy-based frying pan over a moderate heat, turning or stirring frequently, for 5 minutes or until golden. Allow the nuts to cool a little, then chop them roughly. Put the basil, garlic and chopped hazelnuts in a food processor and process to a coarse paste. With the motor running, gradually add the 3 tablespoons of olive oil. Add the flesh of the peppers and chillies and process again until the pesto sauce is smooth.

◆ Bring a large saucepan of water to the boil and cook the linguine according to the instructions on the packet. Drain, return the linguine to the saucepan and add the pesto and a little olive oil. Toss well and season with salt and pepper. Scatter fresh basil over the top and serve.

EACH SERVING CONTAINS
Kcals 575 • Protein 15g • Fat 23g (of which saturated 2.5g) • Carbohydrate 82g
Fibre 8g • Kcals from fat 35% • Excellent source of vitamins C, A and E

Fresh Ginger and Basil Pasta

One of the great advantages of vegan cooking is that the flavours of fresh herbs and roots like garlic and ginger are not masked by dairy products. They remain clean, crisp and fresh. Wherever and whenever possible I eat garlic and ginger in their most effective state: raw. Garlic is especially good for improving the body's immune system.

Serves 4
Preparation time: 10 minutes
Cooking time: 10 minutes, depending on the type of pasta

1 tablespoon peeled, roughly chopped fresh root ginger

1 tablespoon fresh coriander leaves

3 tablespoons fresh basil leaves

2 tablespoons finely chopped garlic

1 tablespoon groundnut oil

2 teaspoons sesame oil

340g (12oz) pasta of your choice

Maldon salt and freshly ground black pepper

handful of fresh basil leaves, roughly torn, to serve

◆ Put the ginger, coriander, basil, garlic and groundnut and sesame oils in a food processor and process until smooth. Season with salt and pepper. Set the sauce aside.

◆ Bring a large saucepan of water to the boil and cook the pasta according to the instructions on the packet. Drain, return the pasta to the saucepan and add the sauce. Toss well. Scatter fresh basil over the top and serve.

EACH SERVING CONTAINS
Kcals 335 • Protein 10g • Fat 6g (of which saturated 1g) • Carbohydrate 64g
Fibre 2.5g • Kcals from fat 16%

Roast Vine Tomatoes and Pasta

Roasting tomatoes with a little citrus juice gives them a completely new identity. This recipe is for a pasta dish, but the tomatoes are just as successful squashed on to slices of hot toast and served as a starter.

Serves 4
Preparation time: 20 minutes
Cooking time: 30 minutes

2 tablespoons olive oil

6 small pickling onions, peeled

2 teaspoons soft light brown sugar

280g (10oz) vine-ripened baby plum
  tomatoes *or* cherry tomatoes,
  quartered

juice of ½ lime

340g (12oz) pasta of your choice

Maldon salt and freshly ground
  black pepper

◆ Preheat the oven to 225°C/425°F/Gas 7. Heat the oil in a frying pan and fry the onions over a moderate heat for about 5 minutes until they start to brown. Sprinkle the sugar over the onions and fry for another 10 minutes. Leave to cool a little, then cut the onions in half. Transfer them to a shallow ovenproof dish. Place the tomatoes on top and drizzle the lime juice over them. Roast in the oven for 15 minutes.

◆ Bring a large saucepan of water to the boil and cook the pasta according to the instructions on the packet. Drain, return the pasta to the saucepan and add the sauce. Toss well and season with salt and pepper. Serve immediately.

EACH SERVING CONTAINS
Kcals 375 • Protein 11g • Fat 7g (of which saturated 3g) • Carbohydrate 70g
Fibre 6g • Kcals from fat 17% • Excellent source of vitamins C and A

Summer Pasta Salad

This may seem very simple but I expect that many of you will cook it over and over again. I love meals like this one, especially when time is short and I need a recipe that happily accepts any fresh vegetables that happen to be in the fridge. Add the dressing to the hot pasta so that it absorbs the fresh mint and lemon flavours.

Serves 4
Preparation time: 15 minutes
Cooking time: 10–12 minutes

340g (12oz) 'spirali' pasta

100g (3½oz) baby corn, halved lengthways

100g (3½oz) sugarsnap peas, halved lengthways

½ cucumber, unpeeled

115g (4oz) black olives, pitted

6 medium-sized vine-ripened tomatoes, quartered; choose ripe, juicy ones

Maldon salt and freshly ground black pepper

handful of fresh mint leaves, roughly chopped, to serve

For the dressing

4 tablespoons olive oil

juice of 1 lemon

2 tablespoons fresh mint leaves, roughly chopped

Maldon salt and freshly ground black pepper

◆ Make the dressing: Put all the ingredients in a screw-top jar and shake vigorously until well blended. Set aside.

◆ Bring a large saucepan of water to the boil and cook the pasta according to the instructions on the packet. Drain, and put into a warm serving dish.

◆ Meanwhile, bring a small saucepan of water to the boil. Add the baby corn and sugarsnap peas and blanch for 2 minutes. Drain and add to the pasta. Add the dressing to the hot pasta and toss until it is well coated.

◆ Cut the cucumber in half lengthways and scoop out the seeds with a teaspoon. Cut the cucumber into very thin strips using a vegetable peeler. Add the cucumber, olives and tomatoes to the pasta. Toss well to mix. Divide the pasta between 4 warm plates and season with salt and pepper. Scatter fresh mint over the top and serve.

EACH SERVING CONTAINS
Kcals 480 • Protein 13g • Fat 16g (of which saturated 2.5g) • Carbohydrate 74g • Fibre 6g
Kcals from fat 31% • Excellent source of vitamin C

Rich Mushroom Sauce with Tagliatelle

This is a quick pasta dish provided you remember to soak the porcini beforehand. It is quite exciting watching the dried mushrooms come back to life as they absorb the water. If you ever use them in a recipe that does not require the soaking liquor, pour it into ice-cube trays and freeze it – it is too good to be wasted. You can use a couple of cubes in soups or sauces to add a quick burst of flavour.

Serves 4
Preparation time: 20 minutes, plus soaking time
Cooking time: 30 minutes

15g (½oz) dried porcini
300ml (10fl oz) boiling water
1 tablespoon olive oil
½ medium-sized onion, finely
  chopped
1 garlic clove, crushed
550g (1¼lb) field mushrooms, finely
  chopped

1 tablespoon Marsala *or* brandy
  (optional)
340g (12oz) tagliatelle
handful of fresh flat-leaf parsley,
  roughly chopped
Maldon salt and freshly ground
  black pepper

◆ Cover the porcini with the boiling water and leave to soak for 30 minutes.

◆ Heat the oil in a frying pan, and sauté the onion over a moderate heat for 5 minutes until soft and golden. Add the garlic and sauté for a further 1 minute. Drain the porcini and reserve the soaking liquid. Chop the porcini finely. Add the porcini and field mushrooms to the onion. Cook over a low heat for 20 minutes, then add the reserved soaking liquid and Marsala or brandy, if using. Turn up the heat and simmer for 5 minutes or until the liquid has reduced slightly.

◆ Bring a large saucepan of water to the boil and cook the tagliatelle according to the instructions on the packet. Drain, return the pasta to the saucepan and add the sauce and parsley. Season with salt and pepper, toss well and serve.

EACH SERVING CONTAINS
Kcals 365 • Protein 14g • Fat 5g (of which saturated 1g) • Carbohydrate 67g
Fibre 5g • Kcals from fat 13% • Good source of niacin

Vivid Beetroot and Horseradish Gnocchi

Beetroot needs to be handled and cooked with care – its wonderful vivid colour will leach out into the water if it is boiled. In a dish like this the colour is vitally important so I roast the beetroot with their skins on and peel them before puréeing. The result is a fabulous bright red sauce with a wonderful flavour and texture. It goes as well with pasta or polenta as it does with gnocchi.

Serves 4
Preparation time: 20 minutes
Cooking time: 2 hours

450g (1lb) raw beetroot, unpeeled

1 red onion, chopped

sprig of fresh rosemary

sprig of fresh thyme

2 lemon quarters

1 tablespoon olive oil

5cm (2in) piece fresh horseradish
   root, peeled and grated

340g (12oz) gnocchi

Maldon salt and freshly ground
   black pepper

handful of fresh thyme leaves, to
   serve

♦ Preheat the oven to 160°C/325°F/Gas 3. Trim the beetroot and put them in a roasting pan with the onion, herbs and lemon quarters. Drizzle the olive oil over them and season well with salt and pepper. Cover the pan with foil and roast for 2 hours. Leave to cool.

♦ Slip the skins off the beetroot (they should come off easily) and cut the flesh of half of them into chunks. Put the chunks in a food processor and process to a purée. Finely chop the remaining flesh and add it to the purée. Season to taste with salt and pepper and add horseradish to taste. Transfer the purée to a saucepan and warm through gently.

♦ Bring a large saucepan of water to the boil and cook the gnocchi according to the instructions on the packet. Remove the gnocchi with a slotted spoon and divide them between 4 warm plates. Top with the beetroot sauce, scatter thyme leaves over each serving and serve.

EACH SERVING CONTAINS
Kcals 215 • Protein 5g • Fat 3g (of which saturated 0.5g) • Carbohydrate 40g
Fibre 2.5g • Kcals from fat 14% • Good source of folic acid

Samosas with Mango Chutney

*Filo pastry is great to cook with because of its light, crisp texture.
However, it is incredibly thin and consequently will dry out if exposed
to the air. The trick is to keep the sheets covered with a clean damp
cloth until you are ready to use them.*

Serves 4
Preparation time: 20 minutes
Cooking time: about 35 minutes

2 medium-sized ripe tomatoes

2 teaspoons cumin seeds

1 teaspoon coriander seeds

450g (1lb) potatoes, peeled

2 tablespoons vegetable oil

2 large onions, sliced

2 green chillies, seeded and finely
    sliced

2 garlic cloves, crushed

50g (1¾oz) peas

handful of fresh coriander leaves,
    finely chopped

handful of fresh mint leaves, finely
    chopped

4 filo pastry sheets, thawed if
    frozen

vegetable oil, for deep-frying

mango chutney, to serve

◆ Put the tomatoes in a bowl and cover with boiling water. Leave them for
exactly 20 seconds then plunge them straight into cold water. Drain and
skin the tomatoes, then dice their flesh.

◆ Dry-fry the cumin and coriander seeds in a heavy-based frying pan over a
moderate heat, turning or stirring frequently, for a couple of minutes or
until they start to pop and turn golden. Crush coarsely using a pestle and
mortar.

◆ Bring a saucepan of water to the boil, add the potatoes and simmer for
about 15 minutes until tender. Drain the potatoes and chop them into
small pieces.

◆ While the potatoes are boiling, heat the oil in a frying pan and fry the
onions, chillies and garlic over a moderate heat for 5 minutes until the
onions are soft and golden. Add the crushed cumin and coriander and fry
for a further 2 minutes. Add the tomatoes, peas, potatoes, chopped
coriander and mint and fry for a further 2 minutes. Remove the filling from
the heat and leave to cool.

♦ Cut a sheet of filo pastry in half widthways and cover the other 3 sheets and the remaining half with a clean, damp cloth. Put 1 tablespoon of the filling in the centre of the right-hand side of the half-sheet. Bring one corner of the sheet over the filling, then roll the pastry and filling over twice, to make a triangle. Seal the edges with a little water. Repeat with the remaining filo pastry and filling to make a total of 8 samosas.

♦ Half-fill a deep-fryer or heavy-based deep saucepan with the vegetable oil and heat to 180°C (350°F). To test the temperature, drop a cube of bread in the oil – it should brown within 2 minutes. Drop 2 samosas into the oil and deep fry for 5–7 minutes until golden brown. Drain on kitchen paper. Repeat with the remaining samosas. Serve the samosas with a bowl of mango chutney as an accompaniment.

EACH SERVING CONTAINS
Kcals 200 • Protein 5g • Fat 6.5g (of which saturated 0.5g) • Carbohydrate 31g
Fibre 3g • Kcals from fat 30%

Purée of Beans and Potatoes with Olive Oil

If you have ever been to Nîmes in Provence there is a strong chance you will be familiar with this dish. It is a joy to eat – both comforting and delicious – and very simple to make. Serve it with a few fresh green vegetables as a main course. Once again I have sneaked in some raw garlic – it is so good for you.

Serves 4
Preparation time: 10 minutes
Cooking time: 20 minutes

420g (15oz) can white beans, drained

2 medium-sized potatoes, peeled and cut into chunks

1 bay leaf

2 tablespoons olive oil

1 medium-sized onion, sliced

3 garlic cloves, crushed

juice of ½ lemon

pinch of cayenne pepper

♦ Coarsely mash the beans in a bowl. Bring a saucepan of water to the boil, add the potato chunks and bay leaf and simmer for about 15 minutes until the potato is tender. Drain, discard the bay leaf and return the saucepan to the heat. Dry the potato over a very low heat, shaking gently, then mash it.

♦ While the potato is boiling, heat the olive oil in a frying pan and fry the onion and 2 crushed garlic cloves for 2 minutes. Add the mashed beans and mashed potato and mix to a purée. Warm the purée through over a low heat, stirring every now and then to make sure it doesn't stick to the pan.

♦ Remove the purée from the heat and beat in the remaining crushed garlic and the lemon juice. Season to taste with cayenne pepper and serve immediately.

EACH SERVING CONTAINS
Kcals 215 • Protein 11g • Fat 6g (of which saturated 0.9g)
Carbohydrate 30g • Fibre 7g • Kcals from fat 27%

Mediterranean galette

Baking the pastry before adding the topping ensures that you have a crisp, light base underneath the soft vegetables. Tapenade is a spicy paste made from olives and capers and adds lots of flavour as well as acting as a barrier between the pastry and vegetables. It is available from major supermarkets.

Serves 4
Preparation time: 20 minutes
Cooking time: 20 minutes

375g (13oz) sheet puff pastry,
   thawed if frozen
2 tablespoons olive oil
1 red onion, sliced
1 courgette, finely sliced
1 red pepper, seeded and finely
   sliced

2 field mushrooms, thinly sliced
2 tablespoons tapenade
Maldon salt and freshly ground
   black pepper
handful of fresh basil leaves,
   roughly torn, to serve

◆ Preheat the oven to 200°C/400°F/Gas 6. Use an upturned plate or flan tin to cut a 20cm (8in) circle of pastry, then prick the whole surface evenly with a fork. Heat a baking sheet in the oven for 2–3 minutes. Scatter a few drops of water over the hot baking sheet and put the pastry circle on top. Bake for 10–15 minutes until golden and puffy. The drops of water will turn to steam in the hot oven and help the pastry to rise. Turn the pastry over and return it to the oven for 5 minutes.

◆ Meanwhile, heat the oil in a frying pan, add the onion, courgette and red pepper and fry over a moderate heat for 10 minutes until the vegetables have softened. Add the mushrooms, season well with salt and pepper and sauté for a further 5 minutes.

◆ Spread the tapenade over the pastry base, spoon the vegetables over it and return the galette to the oven for 5 minutes. Scatter fresh basil over the top and serve warm.

EACH SERVING CONTAINS
Kcals 440 • Protein 7g • Fat 29g (of which saturated 19g) • Carbohydrate 40g
Fibre 2g • Kcals from fat 59% • Excellent source of vitamins C and A

Fennel and Ginger Tarts

Make sure you roll the pastry thin so that the end result is crisp with a soft sticky centre. If you are lucky enough to find fennel bulbs that still have their feathery fronds, chop the fronds finely and scatter them over the tarts at the end of cooking. Otherwise use dill – it comes from the same family as fennel and the taste is not dissimilar. Choose pale green young fennel bulbs. Reserve any trimmings left over after preparing the bulbs and add them to a vegetable stock (see page 55). Serve the tarts with a green salad and chunks of fresh lemon.

Serves 4
Preparation time: 15 minutes
Cooking time: 30 minutes

225g (8oz) ready-made shortcrust
    pastry, thawed if frozen
5 large fennel bulbs
2 tablespoons extra virgin olive oil
2.5cm (1in) piece fresh root ginger,
    peeled and cut into thin
    matchsticks

Maldon salt and freshly ground
    black pepper

To serve
handful of fennel fronds, finely
    sliced
1 lemon, cut into chunks

◆ Preheat the oven to 180°C/350°F/Gas 4. Lightly grease four 10cm (4in) pastry tins. Roll out the pastry to a thickness of about 3mm (⅛in) and cut 4 circles slightly bigger than the tins. Line the tins with the pastry and prick the bases with a fork. Chill in the fridge for 10 minutes.

◆ Line the pastry cases with greaseproof paper and baking beans and bake blind for 10–15 minutes until golden and slightly crispy.

◆ Trim the tough stalks off the fennel bulbs, shave off the bases and remove any damaged outer layers. Slice each bulb in half vertically, cut out the core and slice the bulb into 5–7 strips. Heat the oil in a frying pan, add the ginger and fennel and fry gently for 20 minutes or until the fennel is soft and caramelized. Season with salt and pepper. You may have to do this in 2 batches depending on the size of the frying pan: the fennel will steam and not get brown if the pan is too small. Spoon the caramelized fennel into the pastry cases and return to the oven for 5 minutes.

◆ Scatter the fennel fronds over the tarts. Serve warm with chunks of lemon.

EACH SERVING CONTAINS
Kcals 320 • Protein 4.5g • Fat 21g (of which saturated 6.5g)
Carbohydrate 29g • Fibre 4.5g • Kcals from fat 60%

Four-Onion Croustades

I once made a five-onion tart on television and not one member of the audience could name all of them. They were amazed to learn that chives and garlic are both members of the onion family. Since then I have experimented with soups, tarts and pizzas that contain a number of different onions. Combining them in one dish always seems to work really well as they complement one another in flavour, colour and texture. Although onions contain a lot of natural sugar, I have added a little brown sugar to speed the caramelization process along a little. The little bread cups are excellent for serving vegetables. For a sweet version, use a good fruity bread for the croustades and dust with cinnamon and sugar before baking. Fill them with poached fruits.

Serves 4
Preparation time: 20 minutes
Cooking time: 45 minutes

8 medium slices white bread, crusts removed	1 tablespoon chopped chives
3 tablespoons vegetable oil	1 tablespoon soft brown sugar
2 medium leeks	Maldon salt and freshly ground black pepper
1 garlic clove, crushed	handful of fresh chives, finely
1 Spanish onion, sliced	chopped, to serve

◆ Preheat the oven to 160°C/325°F/Gas 3. Lightly oil 8 patty (tart) pans. Flatten the bread slices with a rolling pin. Brush both sides of each slice with oil and season with salt and pepper. Press the slices into the patty pans. Bake for 40 minutes until crisp and golden.

◆ Meanwhile, chop each leek into 4 pieces, then cut each piece into long thin strips. Heat about 1½ tablespoons oil in a frying pan and add the garlic, leeks, onion and chives. Sauté over a moderate heat for 5 minutes until the vegetables are softened. Add the sugar, cover and sauté for a further 10 minutes or until the onions have caramelized. Season to taste with salt and pepper.

◆ Spoon the caramelized onions into the crispy croustades and heat through in the oven for 5 minutes. Scatter fresh chives over the top and serve immediately.

EACH SERVING CONTAINS
Kcals 270 • Protein 7g • Fat 9g (of which saturated 1g) • Carbohydrate 41g
Fibre 2.5g • Kcals from fat 33%

Warm Tomato and Aubergine Stacks

So often very basic recipe ideas can be transformed into masterpieces by the way they are presented. These stacks are little towers of purple, green and red with a delicious dressing dribbling down the sides and a flourish of fresh herbs scattered over the top.

Serves 4
Preparation time: 20 minutes
Cooking time: 20 minutes

4 beef tomatoes

olive oil, for griddling

1–2 small aubergines, cut into eight
   1cm (½in) slices

2 courgettes, cut into 1cm (½in)
   slices

handful of fresh basil leaves,
   roughly torn, to serve

For the dressing

1 garlic clove

pinch of Maldon salt

juice and zest of 1 large lemon

6 tablespoons extra virgin olive oil

2 tablespoons finely chopped fresh
   mint leaves

freshly ground black pepper

◆ Preheat the oven to 190°C/375°F/Gas 5. Score a cross in the top of each tomato, put them in a bowl and cover with boiling water. Leave them for exactly 20 seconds then plunge them straight into cold water. Drain and skin the tomatoes, then cut each one into 4 thick slices.

◆ Brush a griddle pan or heavy-based frying pan with olive oil and heat until very hot. Griddle the aubergine slices for 4 minutes on each side. Griddle the courgette slices for 1 minute on each side.

◆ Put 4 aubergine slices on to a lightly oiled baking tray and layer the courgette and tomato slices on top to make little stacks. Finish each stack with an aubergine slice, secure with a cocktail stick and bake in the oven for 10 minutes.

◆ Meanwhile make the dressing: Crush the garlic with a pinch of salt using a pestle and mortar. Add the lemon zest and juice and whisk with a fork until well mixed. Gradually whisk the oil into the garlic mixture. Season with pepper and stir in the mint.

◆ Remove the cocktail sticks from the stacks and spoon the dressing over the top. Scatter fresh basil over the stacks and serve hot.

EACH SERVING CONTAINS
Kcals 220 • Protein 3g • Fat 20g (of which saturated 3g) • Carbohydrate 7g
Fibre 4g • Kcals from fat 84% • Excellent source of vitamin C

Warm Lemon and Olive Oil Beans on Rosemary Mash

These warmed beans with oil and watercress are very simple and extremely effective. I love to infuse oils with herbs and garlic, especially when recipes use tough herbs like rosemary. It's a great way to add their flavour to a dish without adding the herb.

Serves 4
Preparation time: 10 minutes
Cooking time: about 20 minutes

5 tablespoons extra virgin olive oil

3 sprigs of fresh rosemary

1 garlic clove

900g (2 lb) potatoes, peeled and cut into chunks

zest of ½ lemon

two 400g (14oz) cans borlotti beans *or* cannellini beans, drained

juice of 1 lemon

handful of fresh parsley, roughly chopped

30g (1oz) bunch of watercress, roughly chopped

Maldon salt and freshly ground black pepper

♦ Heat 2 tablespoons olive oil in a frying pan, add the rosemary and garlic and heat gently for 2 minutes. Remove from the heat, cover, and leave to infuse while you prepare the mashed potatoes.

♦ Bring a saucepan of water to the boil, add the potato chunks and simmer for about 15 minutes until the potatoes are tender. Drain and return the saucepan to the heat. Dry the potatoes over a very low heat, shaking the pan gently.

♦ Remove the rosemary sprigs and garlic from the oil with a slotted spoon and discard. Add the oil and lemon zest to the potatoes and mash until they are smooth and creamy. Keep warm.

♦ Put the beans in a saucepan, drizzle the remaining olive oil and the lemon juice over them and warm through over a gentle heat. Stir in the parsley and watercress, season well with salt and pepper and warm through again.

♦ Divide the rosemary mash between 4 warm plates, put the beans on top and serve immediately.

EACH SERVING CONTAINS
Kcals 448 • Protein 17g • Fat 15g (of which saturated 2g) • Carbohydrate 64g
Fibre 12g • Kcals from fat 31% • Good source of vitamin C

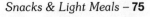

Warm Cumin and Coriander Spinach on Garlic Mash

Comfort food in a bowl. I adore cumin and coriander seeds roasted and ground and mixed through fresh spinach. Their flavour is fabulous and doesn't mask that of the spinach. If you don't have time to mash potatoes, serve the spinach with fresh bread for mopping up the juices.

Serves 4
Preparation time: 15 minutes
Cooking time: 25 minutes

900g (2lb) floury potatoes, peeled
   and cut into chunks
1 garlic clove
5 tablespoons olive oil
2 tablespoons whole-grain mustard
   (optional)
1 teaspoon cumin seeds

1 teaspoon coriander seeds
2 red onions, finely sliced
400g (14oz) fresh spinach leaves
juice of ½ lemon
Maldon salt and freshly ground
   black pepper
lemon wedges, to serve

♦ Bring a saucepan of water to the boil, add the potato chunks and simmer for about 15 minutes until tender. Drain and return the saucepan to the heat. Dry the potatoes over a very low heat, shaking the pan gently.

♦ Using a pestle and mortar, crush the garlic with 2 tablespoons olive oil and a pinch of salt. Add the garlic oil to the potatoes and mash until they are smooth and creamy. Stir in the mustard, if using, and season well with salt and pepper. Keep warm.

♦ Dry-fry the cumin and coriander seeds over a moderate heat in a heavy-based frying pan, stirring frequently, for a couple of minutes until they start to pop and go golden. Coarsely crush the seeds using a pestle and mortar.

♦ Heat the remaining oil in a large saucepan, add the onions and cook gently for 10 minutes until they are soft but not coloured. Add the crushed spices and fry, stirring, for 1 minute. Add the spinach leaves, cover and cook for a couple of minutes until they wilt. Season with salt and pepper. Add the lemon juice and toss until the leaves are well coated.

♦ Divide the garlic mash between 4 warm bowls, top with the spicy spinach and serve with lemon wedges.

EACH SERVING CONTAINS
Kcals 345 • Protein 8g • Fat 15g (of which saturated 2g) • Carbohydrate 46g • Fibre 6g
Kcals from fat 40% • Excellent source of vitamin A • Good source of iron, vitamin C, folic acid

Red Cabbage Relish with Parsley Mash

A little balsamic vinegar and a few sweet fruits like apples and sultanas can transform the humble cabbage. This dish always makes me think of Christmas – if you are the same you may like to join me in topping it with a large spoonful of cranberry relish. You could even add a handful of dried cranberries to the dish.

Serves 4
Preparation time: 15minutes
Cooking time: 25 minutes

675g (1½lb) red cabbage

3 tablespoons olive oil

2 tablespoons red wine vinegar

30g (1oz) soft brown sugar

3 tablespoons red wine

2 Cox's apples, peeled, cored and
    thickly sliced

30g (1oz) sultanas

1 bay leaf

900g (2lb) floury potatoes, peeled
    and cut into chunks

2 tablespoons very finely chopped
    fresh flat-leaf parsley

Maldon salt and freshly ground
    black pepper

◆ Remove the outer leaves and core of the cabbage and slice finely. Heat 1 tablespoon olive oil in a saucepan. Stir in the cabbage, then cover and sweat for 5 minutes over a very low heat. Add the vinegar, sugar, wine, apples, sultanas and bay leaf and season with salt and pepper. Mix well. Cover the saucepan and cook gently for 20 minutes or until the cabbage is soft and sticky, but still has a little 'crunch'. Stir frequently to prevent sticking and burning.

◆ Meanwhile, bring a saucepan of water to the boil, add the potato chunks and simmer for about 15 minutes until the potato is tender. Drain and return the saucepan to the heat. Dry the potatoes over a very low heat, shaking the pan gently. Mash the potatoes, then add the parsley and remaining olive oil. Season with salt and pepper. Divide the parsley mash between 4 warm bowls, top with the red cabbage relish and serve.

EACH SERVING CONTAINS
Kcals 350 • Protein 7g • Fat 9g (of which saturated 1g) • Carbohydrate 63g • Fibre 8g
Kcals from fat 24% • Excellent source of vitamin C • Good source of Vitamin B_6, folic acid

Balsamic White Peach Salad with Parsley Shortcakes

I often serve shortcakes instead of bread with salads. The ingredients I use to add flavour to the basic mix depend on the salad. These parsley shortcakes are particularly good filled with the fresh peppery peach salad and its juicy dressing. Replace the parsley with chilli pepper or crushed garlic for slightly different shortcakes that go well with a vegan cheese. The recipe is wonderfully versatile – if sweet ingredients like cinnamon and sugar are substituted for savoury ones, the shortcake can be used to create a tasty dessert.

Serves 4
Preparation time: 20 minutes
Cooking time: 10–12 minutes

75g (2½oz) sesame seeds

4 white peaches

250g (9oz) rocket leaves, roughly torn

250g (9oz) black olives, pitted

4 tablespoons balsamic vinegar

4 tablespoons olive oil

Maldon salt and freshly ground black pepper

For the shortcakes

125g (4½oz) plain flour

1½ teaspoons baking powder

pinch of salt

½ teaspoon baking soda

handful of fresh parsley, roughly chopped

2 tablespoons olive oil

1 tablespoon white wine vinegar

6 tablespoons soya milk

◆ Make the shortcakes: Preheat the oven to 200°C/400°F/Gas 6. Line a baking sheet with baking parchment or brush it lightly with olive oil. Combine the flour, baking powder, salt, baking soda and parsley in a bowl. In a separate bowl, mix together the oil, vinegar and soya milk. Make a well in the middle of the flour, pour in the liquid and quickly mix everything together. Do not overmix: the dough is ready when no bits are left in the bowl. Drop 16 tablespoons of the dough on to the prepared baking sheets, spacing them a few inches apart. Flatten them gently and bake for 10–12 minutes until golden.

◆ While the shortcakes are baking, dry-fry the sesame seeds in a heavy-based frying pan over a moderate heat, tossing or stirring frequently, for a couple of minutes until golden. Peel and stone the peaches and cut them into thin slices. Put the slices in a bowl. Add the rocket leaves and olives.

◆ Mix the vinegar and oil together and season with salt and pepper. Drizzle the dressing over the peaches, add the sesame seeds, and toss to coat the fruit.

◆ While the shortcakes are still warm split each one in half horizontally. Spoon a little peach salad on to one half and top with the other half. Serve with any left-over salad as an accompaniment.

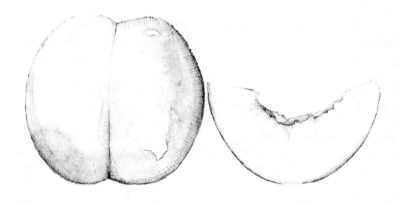

EACH SERVING CONTAINS
Kcals 510 • Protein 10g • Fat 35g (of which saturated 5g) • Carbohydrate 40g • Fibre 7g
Kcals from fat 62% • Excellent source of vitamin C • Good source of iron

Papaya and Coriander Salsa on Coconut Rice

This dish is savoury, sweet, tart, hot and cold all at the same time. Coconut rice is the perfect accompaniment to the salsa, but a soft bread will still make it satisfyingly healthy and tasty. One cup of mango slices contains about three-quarters of the adult daily requirement for vitamins A and C. However, I am still more impressed by our friend the papaya, which has a very clever way of helping us to digest food. In addition, an average-sized papaya provides three times the recommended adult daily requirement for vitamin C, two-thirds of the vitamin A requirement and over one-third of the potassium requirement.

Serves 4
Preparation time: 20 minutes
Cooking time: about 15 minutes

400g (14oz) basmati rice

2 tablespoons coconut cream

1 jalapeño chilli, seeded and finely chopped

2 large ripe papaya

1 large ripe mango

1 red onion, finely sliced

grated zest and juice of 2 limes

2 handfuls of fresh coriander leaves, roughly chopped

◆ Bring a large saucepan of water to the boil and add the rice and coconut cream. Simmer for 15 minutes or until the rice is tender.

◆ Meanwhile, put the chilli into a bowl. Peel the papaya, remove their seeds and cut the flesh into bite-sized chunks. Add the papaya to the chilli. Peel the mango and use a sharp knife to slice the flesh away from the stone. Cut the flesh into bite-sized chunks. Add the mango, onion, lime zest and juice and half the coriander leaves to the papaya and mix together well.

◆ Divide the coconut rice between 4 warm bowls and spoon the salsa on top. Scatter the remaining fresh coriander over each serving and serve.

EACH SERVING CONTAINS
Kcals 450 • Protein 9g • Fat 2g (of which saturated 1.5g) • Carbohydrate 97g • Fibre 4g
Kcals from fat 5% • Excellent source of vitamin C • Good source of vitamin A

Griddled Aubergines with Black Olive Dressing

Aubergines have such a satisfying texture – the bigger the slices, the better the dish. Thick ones chargriddle really well. The secret is not to panic when the vegetable initially cries out for oil. Allow it to carry on cooking, however dry it may appear, and it will gradually release its own juices. Because of their bland flavour aubergines need a few pungent additions, hence the sauce of black olives, capers and garlic.

Serves 4
Preparation time: 15 minutes
Cooking time: 10 minutes

---

2 garlic cloves

12 black olives, pitted and roughly chopped

4 teaspoons small capers

handful of fresh flat-leaf parsley, roughly chopped

handful of fresh coriander leaves, roughly chopped

2 tablespoons extra virgin olive oil, plus extra for griddling and drizzling

2 large aubergines, each cut into 4 slices

55g (2oz) mixed baby salad leaves, roughly torn

Maldon salt and freshly ground black pepper

handful of fresh coriander leaves, to serve

◆ Preheat the oven to 200°C/400°F/Gas 6. Crush the garlic using a pestle and mortar, add the chopped olives and the capers and crush to a thick lumpy paste. Add the parsley and coriander, then whisk in the 2 tablespoons of olive oil with a fork.

◆ Brush a griddle pan or heavy-based frying pan with a little olive oil and heat until very hot. Brush the aubergine slices with a little oil. Griddle the slices for about 5 minutes on each side, until charred and cooked. Remove from the pan.

◆ Mix together the salad leaves, drizzle a little extra virgin olive oil over them and season. Divide the leaves between 4 plates, top with the aubergine slices and drizzle the dressing over the top. Serve topped with a few coriander leaves.

EACH SERVING CONTAINS
Kcals 105 • Protein 1.5g • Fat 10g (of which saturated 1.5g) • Carbohydrate 3g
Fibre 3g • Kcals from fat 84%

Fresh Broad Beans with Paprika and Lemon

Broad beans appear quite frequently in Moroccan cookery so I have chosen Moroccan flavours like paprika and lemon for this dish. If fresh beans are not available, use frozen ones, but make sure that you cook them for slightly longer. Serve on toast or with a fresh salad.

Serves 4
Preparation time: 20 minutes
Cooking time: 15 minutes

450g (1lb) fresh broad beans *or*
    frozen broad beans, thawed
1 small onion, finely chopped
3 tablespoons extra virgin olive oil
50g (1¾oz) fresh coriander leaves,
    roughly chopped

1 teaspoon paprika
juice of ½ lemon
Maldon salt and freshly ground
    black pepper
zest of 1 lemon, cut into strips

◆ Shell the beans. Put them in a saucepan, add the onion and olive oil and season with salt and pepper. Cover with water (not more than 250ml/ 7fl oz), bring to the boil and simmer for 10 minutes. Add the coriander leaves, paprika and lemon juice and simmer, covered, for a further 5 minutes or until the beans are tender and the liquid is reduced.

◆ Transfer the beans to a serving dish and garnish with the lemon zest. Serve hot, warm or at room temperature.

EACH SERVING CONTAINS
Kcals 150 • Protein 7g • Fat 9g (of which saturated 1g) • Carbohydrate 10g • Fibre 7g
Kcals from fat 56% • Excellent source of vitamin C • Good source of folic acid

Chilli and Coriander Sweetcorn Fritters with Tomato Sauce

Although I am not a great fan of deep-frying I recognize that many people enjoy a little fritter from time to time and have included a couple of such recipes to satisfy those cravings. To make these fritters a little different, I have included a few chopped and ground almonds to add flavour, crunch and extra protein. The addition of lots of red chillies and fresh coriander ensures that each fritter is packed with colour and flavour. Eat the fritters as soon as they are cooked – they do not improve with age.

Serves 4
Preparation time: 20 minutes
Cooking time: 15 minutes

55g (2oz) almonds

225g (8oz) plain flour

55g (2oz) ground almonds

2 teaspoons salt

340g (12oz) can sweetcorn kernels

3 red chillies, seeded and finely
    chopped

2 teaspoons chilli powder

pinch of freshly ground black
    pepper

2 tablespoons fresh coriander
    leaves, roughly chopped

vegetable oil, for deep-frying

For the tomato sauce

1 tablespoon olive oil

1 shallot, finely sliced

400g (14oz) can tomatoes

1 tablespoon fresh coriander
    leaves, roughly chopped

Maldon salt and freshly ground
    black pepper

◆ Preheat the oven to 150°C/300°F/Gas 2. Line a plate or baking tray with kitchen paper. Make the tomato sauce: Heat the olive oil in a frying pan, add the shallot and sweat over a gentle heat for 2–3 minutes until softened. Add the tomatoes and simmer for 5 minutes. Stir in the coriander and season to taste. Keep warm.

◆ Dry-fry the almonds in a heavy-based frying pan over a moderate heat, tossing or stirring frequently, for 5 minutes until golden. Leave the nuts to cool a little, then chop them.

◆ Put the flour, ground almonds and salt in a food processor. Add 250ml (8½fl oz) water and process to a thick batter. Transfer to a bowl. Add the

▶

sweetcorn kernels, chopped almonds, chillies, chilli powder, pepper and coriander leaves and mix well.

◆ Heat the vegetable oil to about 190°C (375°F) in a deep-fryer or deep, heavy-based saucepan. To test the temperature, drop a little batter into the oil – it should sizzle immediately. Carefully drop a few tablespoons of the mixture into the hot oil and fry for a few minutes until golden brown. Drain on kitchen paper and keep warm in the oven. Repeat the process with the remaining mixture. Serve immediately with the tomato sauce as an accompaniment.

Roasted Potatoes and Parsnips with Chestnuts and Sage

There are so many ingredients that make life easier for the modern cook. Cooked and peeled chestnuts, conveniently vacuum packed to keep the nuts fresh until you want to use them, are an example and are well worth keeping in the storecupboard. Serve these root vegetables in warm bowls with fresh green vegetables, topped with a large spoonful of lingonberry relish in the centre. Substitute a relish made from cranberries if you wish – lingonberries are their Swedish sisters. If you are using old parsnips, remove the woody cores.

Serves 4
Preparation time: 20 minutes
Cooking time: 35–40 minutes

2 tablespoons olive oil
450g (1lb) potatoes, peeled and cut
   into chunks
450g (1lb) parsnips, peeled and cut
   into chunks

200g (7oz) cooked peeled
   chestnuts
2 large handfuls of fresh sage,
   roughly chopped
4 tablespoons relish

◆ Preheat the oven to 225°C/425°F/Gas 7. Heat the olive oil on top of the hob in a heavy-based roasting tin. Add the potatoes and parsnips and sauté them over a high heat for 5 minutes until they start to go brown. Transfer the dish to the oven and roast for 20 minutes. Add the chestnuts and fresh sage and roast for a further 20–25 minutes.

◆ Divide the vegetables between 4 warm bowls, top each serving with a spoonful of lingonberry relish and serve.

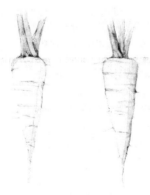

EACH SERVING CONTAINS
Kcals 290 • Protein 5g • Fat 8g (of which saturated 1g) • Carbohydrate 52g • Fibre 8g
Kcals from fat 26% • Good source of vitamin B₁ (thiamine), vitamin C and folic acid

Spanish Potato Gratin

My brother's Spanish girlfriend often comes to stay with us in England. She and I play in the kitchen with ingredients that she is familiar with to create a meal that we both love. This recipe was developed one evening before we rushed off to the cinema. It is one of those dishes that can grow and develop each time it is cooked. You could add peppers – or other vegetables like courgettes and aubergines – to the tomato base. It all depends on the available ingredients and how long you wish to spend in the kitchen. Serve with a fresh green salad.

Serves 4
Preparation time: 15 minutes
Cooking time: 35 minutes

300g (10½oz) potatoes, peeled and
   cut into chunks
3 tablespoons olive oil
1 large onion, sliced
1 garlic clove, finely chopped
400g (14oz) can plum tomatoes,
   roughly chopped
55g (2oz) green olives, pitted

55g (2oz) black olives, pitted
30g (1oz) fresh flat-leaf parsley,
   finely chopped
30g (1oz) fresh thyme leaves, finely
   chopped
75g (2½oz) brown breadcrumbs
Maldon salt and freshly ground
   black pepper

◆ Preheat the oven to 190°C/375°F/Gas 5. Bring a saucepan of water to the boil, add the potato chunks and simmer for about 15 minutes until tender. Drain and return the saucepan to the heat. Dry the potatoes over a very low heat, shaking the pan gently. Mash the potatoes.

◆ Heat half the oil in a large saucepan. Add the onion and garlic and sauté over a moderate heat for 5 minutes or until the onion is soft and golden. Mix in the tomatoes, olives, half the parsley and thyme and season with salt and pepper. Spoon the mixture into an ovenproof dish. Top with the mashed potatoes and scatter the breadcrumbs and remaining parsley and thyme over them. Drizzle the remaining oil over the top and bake in the oven for 15 minutes or until the potatoes are golden. Serve immediately.

EACH SERVING CONTAINS
Kcals 240 • Protein 5g • Fat 12g (of which saturated 2g) • Carbohydrate 28g
Fibre 5g • Kcals from fat 47% • Excellent source of vitamin C

Salad of Ciabatta Croutons with Avocado, Grapefruit and Vinaigrette

The croutons make an excellent crunchy contrast to the soft avocado. Avocados are ripe if they yield when you press the skin gently. Keep them in a fruit bowl if you wish to speed up the ripening process. Once ripe, they can be stored in the fridge.

Serves 4
Preparation time: 15 minutes
Cooking time: 10 minutes

4 slices ciabatta bread, about
   2.5cm (1in) thick

2 tablespoons extra virgin olive oil

2 ripe grapefruit

4 ripe avocados

For the vinaigrette

5 tablespoons extra virgin olive oil

2 tablespoons white wine vinegar

1 teaspoon coarse-grain mustard

Maldon salt and freshly ground
   black pepper

◆ Preheat the oven to 200°C/400°F/Gas 6. Cut the slices of bread into 2.5cm (1in) squares and place these on a baking tray in a single layer. Drizzle the oil over them. Bake in the oven for 10 minutes until golden, turning the croutons once.

◆ Peel the grapefruit, working around the fruit with a sharp knife. Make sure you remove the pith. Then cut the segments of flesh away from the membrane with the knife. Put the segments in a bowl. Slice the avocados in half lengthways and remove the stones. Peel the avocados, then slice the flesh and add it to the grapefruit.

◆ Make the vinaigrette: Put all the ingredients in a screw-top jar and shake vigorously until they are throughly blended. The dressing must be slightly thick.

◆ Drizzle the vinaigrette over the fruit, toss and season well. Add the croutons to the salad and serve.

EACH SERVING CONTAINS
Kcals 535 • Protein 5g • Fat 48g (of which saturated 10g) • Carbohydrate 20g
Fibre 6.5g • Kcals from fat 81% • Excellent source of vitamins C and E

Spicy Satay on White Bread

I love snacks like this one. If you want to make the sandwiches a little more colourful, grate lots of fresh carrot over the satay filling. This peanut spread also makes a fabulous dip – just add a little more water to make it slightly looser in texture.

Serves 4
Preparation time: 5 minutes
Cooking time: 10 minutes

4 tablespoons peanut butter

3 garlic cloves, crushed

1 green chilli, seeded and chopped

50g (1¾oz) creamed coconut

1 tablespoon soy sauce

8 thick slices white bread

2 spring onions, finely sliced

freshly ground black pepper

◆ Put the peanut butter, garlic and chilli into a saucepan with 150ml (5fl oz) water. Heat gently, stirring, until smooth. Add the creamed coconut and soy sauce, season with pepper and mix thoroughly.

◆ Spread a thick layer of the satay on 4 slices of bread. Scatter the spring onions over the satay and cover with the remaining slices of bread.

EACH SERVING CONTAINS
Kcals 375 • Protein 12g • Fat 18g (of which saturated 9g)
Carbohydrate 42g • Fibre 2.5g • Kcals from fat 45%

Red Rice Salad

Red rice has a lovely nutty flavour and texture and a wonderful rusty colour. It is available from most supermarkets but, if you cannot find any, use a mixture of wild and basmati rice instead. The combination of beetroot and horseradish gives this salad a delicious flavour kick. Make the salad in advance and keep it in the fridge. The flavour improves with time, so you could prepare it in the evening for lunch the following day.

Serves 4
Preparation time: 15 minutes
Cooking time: 10–15 minutes

200g (7oz) red rice

7 radishes, thinly sliced

1 red pepper, seeded and cut into
    thin strips

2 medium-sized cooked beetroot,
    cut into small chunks

1 red onion, diced

large handful of fresh chives, finely
    chopped

For the dressing

4 tablespoons white wine vinegar

2 tablespoons creamed
    horseradish

1 tablespoon whole-grain mustard

1 teaspoon caster sugar

1 teaspoon Maldon salt

1 teaspoon freshly ground black
    pepper

4 tablespoons extra virgin olive oil

◆ Cook the rice according to the instructions on the packet. Leave to cool, then transfer to a serving bowl.

◆ Meanwhile, make the dressing: Put all the ingredients in a screw-top jar and shake vigorously until they are throughly blended.

◆ Add the radishes, red pepper, beetroot and onion to the rice and mix well. Scatter the fresh chives over the top. Pour the dressing over the rice, mix well and serve.

EACH SERVING CONTAINS
Kcals 320 • Protein 5g • Fat 12g (of which saturated 1.5g) • Carbohydrate 47g • Fibre 2g
Kcals from fat 34% • Excellent source of vitamin C • Good source of vitamins B_1, niacin, B_6, E

Winter Green Salad with Very Garlicky Vinaigrette

Most of us tend to be lazy when it comes to making fresh green salads. So many bags of mixed leaves are available in supermarkets that we don't spend any time making our own salads. Choose leaves with different flavours, colours and textures and you will be delighted with the finished result. If your supermarket doesn't stock the ones in this recipe, ask your local greengrocer for a selection.

This salad is also good with big, crunchy croutons tossed through it.

Serves 4
Preparation time: 10 minutes

125g (4½oz) arugula leaves
125g (4½oz) watercress
55g (2oz) red leaf lettuce
55g (2oz) romaine leaves
140g (5oz) radicchio
140g (5oz) endive

For the garlicky vinaigrette
3 garlic cloves, crushed
2 tablespoons Dijon mustard
90ml (3fl oz) extra virgin olive oil

◆ Make the garlicky vinaigrette: Put all the ingredients in a screw-top jar and shake vigorously until they are thoroughly blended. Set aside.

◆ Roughly tear the arugula leaves, watercress, red leaf lettuce and romaine leaves and put them into a salad bowl. Finely slice the radicchio and endive, add them to the bowl and mix well.

◆ Pour the dressing over the salad, toss and serve.

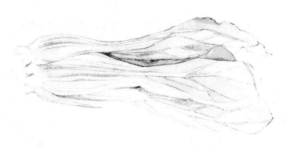

EACH SERVING CONTAINS
Kcals 173 • Protein 2g • Fat 17g (of which saturated 2.5g) • Carbohydrate 2g
Fibre 2g • Kcals from fat 91% • Good source of vitamin C

A Very Modern Waldorf Salad

I have always loved the combination of fruit and nuts and many of my recipes contain both ingredients in many different guises. This salad is easy to make, but very effective. It is often difficult to get the balance of ingredients in a simple recipe right so that the flavours complement, rather than compete with, one another. The crunchy pears and nuts contrast with the soft raisins, and the carrot adds colour as well as being a good source of vitamins. Serve the salad with a fruit bread.

Serves 4
Preparation time: 15 minutes

juice of 1 lemon

4 ripe pears, cored and sliced

4 sticks celery, thinly sliced

3 carrots, grated

125g (4½oz) walnuts, coarsely
   chopped

150g (5½oz) raisins

1 tablespoon fresh mint leaves,
   roughly chopped

For the dressing

2 tablespoons red wine vinegar

1 teaspoon Dijon mustard

4 tablespoons walnut oil

1 tablespoon vegetable oil

Maldon salt and freshly ground
   black pepper

◆ Combine the lemon juice with 120ml (4fl oz) water in a large bowl. Add the pears and toss until they are coated. Leave for 10 minutes then drain.

◆ Make the dressing: Put all the ingredients in a screw-top jar and shake vigorously until they are thoroughly blended. Set aside.

◆ Put the celery, carrots, walnuts and raisins into a serving bowl. Add the pears and fresh mint. Pour the dressing over the salad and serve.

EACH SERVING CONTAINS
Kcals 520 • Protein 6g • Fat 36g (of which saturated 3g) • Carbohydrate 46g • Fibre 7g
Kcals from fat 62% • Excellent source of vitamin A • Good source of vitamin C

If you are looking for sandwich fillings that are more interesting than nut butter or salad, the suggestions on the next few pages are for you. And, of course, many of the dishes in this chapter and the previous one can be adapted to fill sandwiches.

Pitta Breads with Garlic Cream and Fresh Lime

Serves 4
Preparation time: 15 minutes

3 slices white bread, crusts removed

1 tablespoon tahini

2 garlic cloves, crushed

juice of 1 lime

150ml (5fl oz) extra virgin olive oil

2 teaspoons sesame seeds

4 pitta breads, split in half

1 romaine lettuce, finely shredded

handful of fresh mint leaves, roughly chopped

Maldon salt and freshly ground black pepper

1 lime, cut into chunks, to serve

◆ Tear the white bread into chunks. Put the bread, tahini, garlic and lime juice in a food processor and process to a coarse paste. With the motor running, gradually add the olive oil. Transfer the garlic spread to a bowl, season well with salt and pepper and mix in the sesame seeds.

◆ Cut each pitta bread in half widthways, then cut each half open to make 8 pockets. Pack a little lettuce inside each half, spoon a little garlic spread on to the lettuce and scatter some fresh mint over the spread. Serve with wedges of lime.

EACH SERVING CONTAINS
Kcals 540 • Protein 10g • Fat 32g (of which saturated 5g) • Carbohydrate 55g
Fibre 3g • Kcals from fat 54%

Thai Vegetables in Fresh Herb Bread

It is always a refreshing change to make a dressing that has very little oil. If anything really annoys me in restaurants, it is when salads arrive at the table swimming in a tasteless oily dressing. To avoid any embarrassment to the restaurant staff or my friends, I always order dressing on the side so that I can add as much or as little as I like. If you want this one to have more of a kick, add a few seeds from the chillies. The prepared vegetables will keep, covered, in the fridge for at least two hours. I have recommended a herb bread in this recipe, but pumpkin bread or any other speciality bread will do just as well.

Serves 4
Preparation time: 20 minutes

2 carrots, grated

4 spring onions, trimmed and finely
   sliced

125g (4½oz) sugarsnap peas, cut
   into thin strips

125g (4½oz) yellow cherry
   tomatoes, halved

3 tablespoons fresh basil leaves,
   preferably Thai basil

8 slices fresh herb bread

For the dressing

2 red chillies, seeded and finely
   sliced

120ml (4fl oz) coconut milk

juice of 1 lime

2 teaspoons sesame oil

Maldon salt and freshly ground
   black pepper

◆ Mix the carrots, onions, peas and tomatoes in a bowl. Stack 6 basil leaves together, roll them into a cigar shape and cut into thin strips. Add the basil strips to the vegetables. Repeat with the remaining basil.

◆ Put all the dressing ingredients in a screw-top jar and shake vigorously until well blended. Drizzle the dressing over the vegetables, toss well and season to taste with salt and pepper.

◆ Spread the Thai vegetables on 4 slices of bread and cover them with the remaining slices.

EACH SERVING CONTAINS
Kcals 300 • Protein 10g • Fat 6g (of which saturated 3g) • Carbohydrate 54g
Fibre 3.5g • Kcals from fat 18% • Good source of vitamins C and A

Avocado Butter with Tomato Relish in Focaccia

It is almost worth making a double quantity of this fabulous tomato relish and storing some in the fridge to go in other sandwiches or to serve with vegetable dishes – it will keep for at least two days (much longer without the herbs). To transform the avocado butter into a dip, add a skinned and chopped ripe tomato, a few tablespoons of soya yogurt and a little more lime juice to the mixture. You may also need to add a little more Tabasco sauce as the dip should have a bit of a kick to it. Sun blush tomatoes are a pleasing combination of semi-dried tomatoes, garlic and oil and are available in supermarkets.

Serves 4
Preparation time: 20 minutes

For the tomato relish

15 sun blush tomatoes *or* sun-dried
   tomatoes, finely diced
2 garlic cloves, crushed
large handful of fresh basil leaves
large handful of fresh thyme leaves,
   finely chopped
about 2 tablespoons extra virgin
   olive oil

For the avocado butter

2 ripe avocados
juice of ½ lime
1–2 dashes of Tabasco sauce
Maldon salt and freshly ground
   black pepper
4 small focaccia breads *or* 2 large
   focaccia breads, halved

◆ Make the tomato relish: Put the tomatoes and garlic into a bowl. Stack 6 basil leaves together, roll them into a cigar shape and slice into thin strips. Repeat with the remaining basil leaves. Mix the basil and thyme into the tomatoes. Stir in enough oil to make a relish texture.

◆ Make the avocado butter: Slice the avocado in half lengthways and remove the stone. Peel the avocado, then chop the flesh and put it in a food processor. Add the lime juice, Tabasco sauce to taste and season with salt and pepper. Process until smooth.

◆ Cut each focaccia or half focaccia in half widthways. Spread a layer of avocado butter on 4 halves, top with the tomato relish and cover with the remaining halves.

EACH SERVING CONTAINS
Kcals 445 • Protein 2g • Fat 36g (of which saturated 5.5g) • Carbohydrate 24g
Fibre 2.5g • Kcals from fat 72% • Excellent source of vitamin E

Carrots with Pomegranate Syrup in Pitta Breads

Pomegranate syrup is made from the concentrated juice of pomegranates and is a wonderful ingredient to keep in the storecupboard. You only need a little to give a dish a completely new and interesting flavour. If you wish, you can spread a little Puréed Chick Peas (see page 31) in the pitta pockets before adding the salad.

Serves 4
Preparation time: 10 minutes

675g (1½lb) carrots, coarsely
  grated
1 tablespoon olive oil
2 tablespoons pomegranate syrup
large handful of fresh mint leaves,
  roughly chopped

Maldon salt and freshly ground
  black pepper
4 pitta breads

◆ Put the carrots in a bowl. Combine the olive oil, pomegranate syrup and mint leaves in a small bowl and season with salt and pepper. Pour the dressing over the carrots and mix well.

◆ Cut each pitta bread in half widthways, then cut each half open to make 8 pockets. Pack the pockets with the carrot salad.

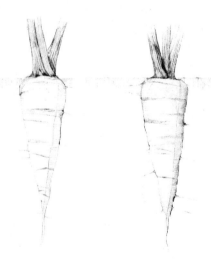

EACH SERVING CONTAINS
Kcals 300 • Protein 8g • Fat 4g (of which saturated 0.7g) • Carbohydrate 62g • Fibre 6g
Kcals from fat 12% • Excellent source of vitamin A • Good source of vitamin C

main courses

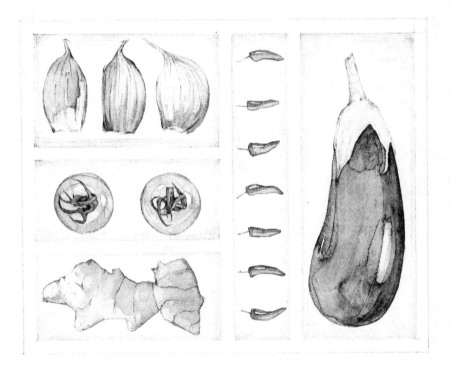

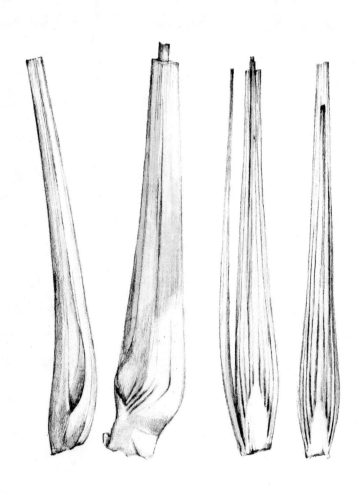

Roasted Garlic Polenta with Sautéed Tomatoes

Roast garlic has a sweet and mellow flavour that is perfect in creamy polenta. Topped with basil and mixed tomatoes dressed with olive oil, it's a dish you will enjoy again and again.

Serves 4
Preparation time: 20 minutes
Cooking time: 55 minutes

---

2 heads of garlic

2 bay leaves

sprig of fresh thyme

3 tablespoons extra virgin olive oil

125g (4½oz) polenta

70g (2½oz) fresh basil leaves

1kg (2¼lb) mixed yellow, cherry
  and plum tomatoes

Maldon salt and freshly ground
  black pepper

◆ Preheat the oven to 180°C/350°F/Gas 4. Bring a saucepan of water to the boil. Slice the heads of garlic in half horizontally, then add them to the boiling water and simmer for about 8 minutes, until they are tender.

◆ Use a draining spoon to drain the garlic and transfer it to an ovenproof dish. Add the bay leaves and thyme, then drizzle 1 tablespoon olive oil over the garlic. Season with salt and pepper and bake for 45 minutes.

◆ Meanwhile, discard the water from the saucepan and rinse out the pan. Pour 600ml (1 pint) water into the pan and add 1 teaspoon salt. Heat until simmering, then add the polenta by letting it run through your fingers in a thin stream while stirring continuously to prevent lumps from forming.

◆ When all the polenta is added, cover the pan and simmer for 30 minutes, stirring every 5 minutes. The polenta is cooked when it comes away from the sides of the saucepan in a smooth thick paste.

◆ Squeeze the flesh out of the garlic and add half to the polenta. Season well and stir in half the basil.

◆ Quarter the large tomatoes and cut the cherry tomatoes in half. Heat the remaining olive oil and garlic flesh in a frying pan over a gentle heat for 1 minute. Add the tomatoes and cook gently for 10 minutes. Add the remaining basil to the tomatoes with salt and pepper to taste. Serve the polenta topped with the hot tomatoes.

EACH SERVING CONTAINS
Kcals 240 • Protein 5g • Fat 10g (of which saturated 1.5g) • Carbohydrate 31g • Fibre 3g
Kcals from fat 38% • Excellent source of vitamins C and A • Good source of vitamin E

Tomato and Pine Nut Linguine with Caramelized Lemon

If you are not familiar with Pomodorino (baby plum) tomatoes, they are sensational. Eating a ripe one is like biting into a sweet. The flavours in this dish are fresh and simple, with hot golden lemon slices to squeeze over the pasta just before you eat it. Serve with French bread.

Serves 4
Preparation time: 15 minutes, plus marinating time
Cooking time: 10–12 minutes

450g (1lb) Pomodorino tomatoes *or* ripe juicy vine-ripened tomatoes, quartered

50g (1¾oz) pine nuts

2 large handfuls of fresh basil leaves

1 tablespoon balsamic vinegar

3 tablespoons light fruity olive oil

400g (14oz) linguine (or other pasta of your choice)

Maldon salt and freshly ground black pepper

½ lemon, thickly sliced from the top

◆ Put the tomatoes in a large bowl and add the pine nuts and half the fresh basil. Drizzle the balsamic vinegar and 2 tablespoons olive oil over the top. Season with salt and lots of pepper and mix well. Leave for at least 30 minutes.

◆ Bring a large saucepan of water to the boil and cook the linguine according to the instructions on the packet. Drain.

◆ While the linguine is cooking, heat the remaining olive oil in a frying pan, and fry the lemon slices for 1 minute on each side or until they start to turn golden.

◆ Add the linguine to the marinated tomatoes and toss well. Scatter the remaining fresh basil over the top and serve with the hot lemon slices.

EACH SERVING CONTAINS
Kcals 535 • Protein 15g • Fat 19g (of which saturated 2g) • Carbohydrate 81g • Fibre 4.5g
Kcals from fat 32% • Excellent source of vitamin C • Good source of vitamins A and E

Gnocchi with Tomatoes and Fresh Mint

The key ingredient in this dish is Rustica crushed tomatoes. Use canned tomatoes if they are unavailable. Remember to check the label on the packet of gnocchi to make sure that they do not contain dairy products.

Serves 4
Preparation time: 10 minutes
Cooking time: 15 minutes

4 tablespoons extra virgin olive oil

1 garlic clove, finely chopped

1 shallot, finely chopped

1 teaspoon golden caster sugar

4 tablespoons vegetable stock

two 350g (12¼oz) jars Cirio Rustica
 crushed tomatoes

400g (14oz) potato gnocchi

Maldon salt and pepper

handful of fresh mint leaves,
 roughly chopped *or* fresh basil
 leaves, torn, to serve

◆ Heat half the olive oil in a frying pan. Add the garlic, shallot, sugar and stock. Cover and cook gently for about 10 minutes or until the onion has softened and the liquid has evaporated. Add the tomatoes, cover and cook for a further 5 minutes. Season to taste with salt and pepper and add the remaining olive oil. Mix well.

◆ Bring a large saucepan of water to the boil and cook the gnocchi for approximately 4 minutes. They will rise to the surface when they are cooked. Remove the gnocchi with a slotted spoon and drain them on kitchen paper while you empty the saucepan. Return the gnocchi to the saucepan, add the sauce and mix well. Scatter fresh mint or basil over the top and serve.

EACH SERVING CONTAINS
Kcals 295 • Protein 6g • Fat 12g (of which saturated 1.5g) • Carbohydrate 42g
Fibre 1g • Kcals from fat 36% • Excellent source of vitamin C

Mixed Mushrooms and Tofu Pasta

The tofu in this recipe adds a little creaminess to coat the pasta. There are many health benefits to eating this soya bean product as it has a high percentage of protein. It is eaten in vast quantities in Japan, along with other products of the bean like shoyu and miso. Try to include a few oriental mushrooms if these are available.

Serves 4
Preparation time: 20 minutes
Cooking time: 20 minutes

500g (1lb 2oz) mixed mushrooms, such as field, button and shiitake

4 garlic cloves, coarsely chopped

1 large onion, sliced

3 tablespoons olive oil

125g (4½oz) pine nuts

2 tablespoons roughly torn fresh basil leaves

2 tablespoons finely chopped fresh thyme leaves

2 tablespoons finely chopped fresh flat-leaf parsley

450g (1lb) firm tofu

juice of ½ lemon

400g (14oz) pasta of your choice

Maldon salt and freshly ground black pepper

handful of mixed fresh basil leaves, fresh thyme leaves and fresh flat-leaf parsley, finely chopped, to serve

◆ Slice large mushrooms into chunks and put the mushrooms, garlic and onion in a food processor. Process to a chunky paste.

◆ Heat the olive oil in a frying pan. Add the mushroom paste and sauté over a moderate heat for 5 minutes. Stir in the pine nuts, basil, thyme and parsley and cook for a further 5 minutes.

◆ Put the tofu in the food processor and process just enough to make a coarse purée – it must not be too creamy. Add the tofu and lemon juice to the mushrooms. Stir well and cook, covered, over a moderate heat for 10 minutes.

◆ Bring a large saucepan of water to the boil and cook the pasta according to the instructions on the packet. Drain, return the pasta to the saucepan and add the mushrooms. Toss well and season with salt and pepper. Divide between 4 warm bowls, scatter fresh basil, thyme and parsley over the top and serve.

EACH SERVING CONTAINS
Kcals 670 • Protein 28g • Fat 28g (of which saturated 2g) • Carbohydrate 80g • Fibre 5g
Kcals from fat 38% • Excellent source of vitamin E • Good source of vitamins B$_1$, niacin

---

Spaghetti with Tomato Sauce

Every vegan book needs a good tomato sauce – and if you are going to do it properly, it should be made with fresh tomatoes (always remove the skins when cooking fresh tomatoes). I have added some sun-dried ones to make the tomato flavour slightly more intense. You could make double the quantity and keep half in the fridge for a few days. It is perfect for serving with vegetables or in lasagnes as well as with spaghetti and other pastas.

Serves 4
Preparation time: 20 minutes
Cooking time: 50 minutes

1 kg (2¼lb) vine-ripened tomatoes	3 sprigs of fresh rosemary
2 tablespoons olive oil	1 teaspoon chilli powder
3 garlic cloves, crushed	pinch of caster sugar
2 large onions	55g (2oz) sun-dried tomatoes,
2 tablespoons fresh basil leaves,	coarsely chopped
roughly chopped	400g (14oz) spaghetti
2 tablespoons fresh thyme leaves,	Maldon salt and freshly ground
chopped	black pepper

◆ Put the tomatoes in a bowl and cover with boiling water. Leave them for exactly 20 seconds then plunge them straight into cold water. Drain and skin the tomatoes then roughly chop their flesh.

◆ Heat the oil in a large saucepan. Add the garlic and onions and sauté over a moderate heat for 5 minutes until soft and golden. Add the tomatoes, basil, thyme, rosemary and chilli powder and simmer gently, uncovered, for about 45 minutes until reduced to a thick sauce, stirring occasionally. Mix in the sugar and season to taste with salt and pepper. Add the sun-dried tomatoes and heat through for a few minutes. Remove the rosemary sprigs.

◆ Bring a large saucepan of water to the boil and cook the spaghetti according to the instructions on the packet. Drain. Divide the spaghetti between 4 warm bowls, spoon the tomato sauce over the top and serve.

EACH SERVING CONTAINS
Kcals 525 • Protein 15g • Fat 15g (of which saturated 2g) • Carbohydrate 88g
Fibre 6g • Kcals from fat 26% • Good source of vitamins C, A and E

Roasted Garlic and Walnut Linguine

My father lived in Rome for three years and I frequently flew to Italy to see him. This dish is based on one of the most memorable vegan meals we ate together. There may seem to be a lot of garlic, but do not panic – the flavour is sweet and subtle after 1½ hours of roasting.

Serves 4
Preparation time: 20 minutes
Cooking time: 1¾ hours

---

2 heads of garlic

4 tablespoons vegetable stock (see page 55)

2 tablespoons olive oil

75g (2½oz) walnuts, roughly chopped

1 tablespoon ground walnuts

2 tablespoons fresh flat-leaf parsley, roughly chopped

400g (14oz) linguine

Maldon salt and freshly ground black pepper

◆ Preheat the oven to 180°C/350°F/Gas 4. Cut the heads of garlic in half widthways and put them in a roasting tin. Drizzle the stock over the garlic and roast for 1¼–1½ hours until soft and tender. Squeeze all the garlic flesh out of the cloves. Mash half the flesh with 1 tablespoon olive oil to make a purée. Reserve the remaining flesh.

◆ Put the walnuts on a baking tray in a single layer and roast for 5 minutes, turning once.

◆ Heat the remaining oil in a large saucepan. Add the garlic purée and ground walnuts and sauté over a moderate heat for 5 minutes. Add the roasted walnuts, remaining garlic and parsley. Season with salt and pepper.

◆ Bring a large saucepan of water to the boil and cook the linguine according to the instructions on the packet. Drain. Toss the linguine with the garlic and walnut sauce and heat gently to warm through. Divide between 4 warm bowls and serve immediately.

EACH SERVING CONTAINS
Kcals 440 • Protein 13.5g • Fat 11g (of which saturated 1.5g) • Carbohydrate 76g
Fibre 3.5g • Kcals from fat 23%

Thai Noodles with Chilli and Lemon Grass Dressing

I would rather the vegetables in this recipe remained raw, to gain the maximum nutritional benefit, but have blanched them as a compromise. Lemon grass will really make the dish sing, but if you do not have any, use lemon zest with a little grated fresh root ginger.

Serves 4
Preparation time: 15 minutes
Cooking time: 10 minutes

250g (9oz) packet dried medium noodles

200g (7oz) asparagus, trimmed

125g (4½oz) mangetout

2 carrots, finely sliced

1 red chilli, seeded and finely sliced

3 spring onions, finely sliced

50g (1¾oz) cashew nuts, chopped

1 red chilli, seeded and finely chopped

1 tablespoon sesame oil

2 tablespoons extra virgin olive oil

1 tablespoon soy sauce

juice of 1 lime

Maldon salt and freshly ground black pepper

For the dressing
1 stick lemon grass, finely chopped

handful of fresh coriander leaves, roughly chopped

To serve
1 red chilli, seeded and finely sliced

5 spring onions, sliced lengthways into thin strips

◆ Bring a large saucepan of water to the boil and cook the noodles for 10 minutes. Drain, then rinse them in cold running water. Set aside.

◆ While the noodles are cooking, bring another pan of water to the boil, add the asparagus and blanch for a couple of minutes. Remove the spears with a slotted spoon, plunge them into a bowl of cold water then drain and slice diagonally. Blanch the mangetout in the same way for 1 minute. Drain.

◆ Make the dressing: Put all the ingredients in a screw-top jar and shake vigorously until well blended.

◆ Put the vegetables, cashew nuts and noodles in a serving bowl. Add the dressing and toss together well. Scatter the chilli and spring onion strips over the top and serve.

EACH SERVING CONTAINS
Kcals 405 • Protein 8g • Fat 15g (of which saturated 2.5g) • Carbohydrate 57g • Fibre 3g
Kcals from fat 33% • Good source of vitamins C and A

Red Cabbage with Sake on Rice Noodles

Rice noodles are one of those ingredients that you either love or hate. Prepared correctly, they can be delicious. They take very little time to cook, but it is always advisable to follow the instructions on the packet rather than a recipe as the instructions vary depending on the size of the noodle. Cook the vegetables for as long as you like. Some people enjoy them with a little bite, others prefer them to be soft.

Serves 4
Preparation time: 20 minutes
Cooking time: 25 minutes

2 tablespoons sesame oil

2 garlic cloves, crushed

1 red cabbage, finely sliced

8 spring onions, finely sliced

5 carrots, finely sliced

5 celery sticks

4 tablespoons soy sauce

4 tablespoons sake

350g (12¼oz) rice noodles

1 bunch of chives, finely chopped, to serve

◆ Heat the sesame oil in a saucepan. Add the garlic, cabbage, spring onions, carrots and celery and sauté over a moderate heat for 10 minutes until the vegetables are soft. Stir in the soy sauce and sake and simmer, covered, for a further 15 minutes or until the vegetables are cooked to your taste.

◆ Meanwhile, cook the rice noodles according to the instructions on the packet.

◆ Transfer the noodles to a large warm bowl, spoon the vegetables on top. Scatter fresh chives over them and serve.

EACH SERVING CONTAINS
Kcals 440 • Protein 8g • Fat 7g (of which saturated 1g) • Carbohydrate 85g • Fibre 8g
Kcals from fat 14% • Excellent source of vitamins A and C • Good source of folic acid

Vegan Sushi with Avocado and Cucumber

The great thing about sushi is that it does not have to involve eating lots of fish. You can enjoy sushi made with avocado and cucumber, or other fruits and vegetables. The combination of sweet and sour – sugar and vinegar – works well with rice and fruits or vegetables. These vegan sushi can look really stunning. For a dramatic effect, serve them on a large dark blue or black plate with the accompaniments in little dishes at the centre of the plate.

Serves 4
Preparation time: 20 minutes
Cooking time: 10 minutes, plus standing time

½ cucumber, peeled

2 tablespoons caster sugar

4 tablespoons rice wine vinegar

piece of dashi-konbu

225g (8oz) Japanese sushi rice

1–2 teaspoons wasabi paste

3 tablespoons pickled ginger

1 large avocado

juice of ½ lime

bowls of pickled ginger, soy sauce
and wasabi paste, to serve

◆ Halve the cucumber lengthways and scoop out the seeds with a teaspoon. Slice into thin strips with a vegetable peeler and put in a bowl. Mix the sugar and vinegar in a small bowl and drizzle half the dressing over the cucumber slices. Reserve the remaining dressing.

◆ Put the dashi-konbu, rice and 450ml (15fl oz) water into a large saucepan. Bring to the boil, then remove dashi-konbu, cover, and simmer the rice for 10 minutes until cooked – it should still have a little bite left in it. Remove from the heat and add the remaining dressing. Leave to stand, still covered, for 15 minutes. Transfer the rice to a bowl and leave to cool. Mould the rice into walnut-sized balls and top each ball with a little wasabi and pickled ginger.

◆ Slice the avocado in half lengthways. Remove the stone, peel and slice the flesh into short, thin strips. Drizzle lime juice over the strips. Top each rice ball with an avocado strip or 2 cucumber slices. Arrange the sushi on a large plate and serve with bowls of pickled ginger, soy sauce and wasabi paste.

EACH SERVING CONTAINS
Kcals 315 • Protein 5g • Fat 8g (of which saturated 1.5g) • Carbohydrate 58g
Fibre 2g • Kcals from fat 24%

Tomato and Basil Risotto

Once you know the secret to making a really good risotto it is easy to adapt the ingredients and change its identity completely. The important thing to remember is to add the liquid gradually to the rice. Once cooked, a good risotto should be slightly soupy, not mushy, and the rice should still have a little bite left in it. As with all risottos, keep the stock warm at all times; this way the rice will never stop cooking.

Serves 4
Preparation time: 10 minutes
Cooking time: 20 minutes

350g (12¼oz) jar Cirio Rustica
  crushed tomatoes *or* 350g
  (12¼oz) fresh tomatoes
750ml (1¼ pints) vegetable stock
  (see page 55)
1 tablespoon olive oil

3 shallots, chopped
400g (14oz) arborio rice
1 large bunch of fresh basil leaves,
  roughly torn
Maldon salt and freshly ground
  black pepper

♦ If you are using fresh tomatoes, put them in a bowl and cover with boiling water. Leave them for exactly 20 seconds then plunge them straight into cold water. Drain and skin the tomatoes then dice their flesh.

♦ Heat the stock in a saucepan until just simmering. It must continue to simmer while you cook the rice.

♦ Heat the oil in a large saucepan and gently fry the shallots for 5 minutes or until softened and golden. Add the rice and stir for 2 minutes until well coated. Add 2 ladles of stock and cook, stirring, until the rice has absorbed all the stock. Continue to cook, adding a few ladles of stock at a time, until all the stock has been absorbed and the rice is tender and creamy but still firm to the bite. If more liquid is required, use hot water.

♦ Remove the pan from the heat, season with salt and pepper and stir in the fresh basil. Transfer to a warm serving dish and serve at once.

EACH SERVING CONTAINS
Kcals 430 • Protein 9g • Fat 6.5g (of which saturated 1g) • Carbohydrate 90g
Fibre 1g • Kcals from fat 13%

Caramelized Fennel and Shallot Risotto

If you are fortunate enough to buy fennel bulbs that still have their feathery fronds attached, chop these and scatter them over the risotto at the last minute with the fresh tarragon. The tarragon enhances the fennel's anise-like flavour. I have added a little sugar to help speed up the caramelization process. However, if you prefer your risotto less sweet, leave out the sugar and give the vegetables a little more cooking time to allow the shallots' natural sugars to caramelize.

Serves 4
Preparation time: 10 minutes
Cooking time: 50 minutes

1.2 litres (2 pints) vegetable stock (see page 55)

2 large fennel bulbs, about 450g (1lb) total

2 tablespoons olive oil

3 shallots, sliced

1 tablespoon soft brown sugar

400g (14oz) arborio rice

Maldon salt and freshly ground black pepper

handful of fresh tarragon leaves, roughly chopped

- Heat the stock in a saucepan until just simmering. It must continue to simmer while you cook the risotto.

- Trim the tough stalks off the fennel bulbs, shave off the bases and remove any damaged outer layers. Slice each bulb in half lengthways, cut out the core and slice each half into thin strips.

- Heat the oil in a large saucepan. Add the fennel, shallots and sugar and sauté gently for at least 30 minutes until the vegetables caramelize and go golden and sticky. Put in the rice and stir for 2 minutes until well coated. Add 2 ladles of stock and cook, stirring, until the rice has absorbed all the stock. Continue to cook, adding a few ladles of stock at a time until all the stock has been absorbed and the rice is tender and creamy but still firm to the bite. If more liquid is required, use hot water.

- Remove the pan from the heat and season with salt and pepper. Transfer to a warm serving dish, scatter fresh tarragon over the risotto and serve at once.

EACH SERVING CONTAINS
Kcals 470 • Protein 9g • Fat 9g (of which saturated 2g) • Carbohydrate 93g
Fibre 3g • Kcals from fat 18%

Moroccan Pilaff

The great thing about this dish is that you can pop it in the oven and forget about it until the rice is cooked – just remember to set a timer or you may come back to overcooked grains. I love the way Moroccans use citrus fruits and cinnamon in savoury dishes. It makes a welcome change to dishes like pilaffs that can otherwise seem very similar.

Serves 4
Preparation time: 15 minutes
Cooking time: 45 minutes

2 tablespoons olive oil

50g (1¾oz) whole almonds, roughly
   chopped

1 large onion, chopped

2 carrots, diced

1 cinnamon stick

½ teaspoon ground cinnamon

200g (7oz) long grain rice

50g (1¾oz) currants

50g (1¾oz) dried apricots

grated zest of 1 orange

¼ teaspoon cayenne pepper

Maldon salt and freshly ground
   black pepper

To serve

large handful of fresh coriander
   leaves, roughly chopped

large handful of fresh chives, finely
   chopped

◆ Preheat the oven to 190°C/375°F/Gas 5. Heat the oil in a large flameproof casserole dish, and sauté the almonds over a moderate heat for a few minutes until golden. Add the onion, carrots and cinnamon and sauté for 5 minutes until the onion is soft and golden. Add the rice and cook for 1 minute, stirring, to coat the grains. Stir in the currants, apricots, orange zest and cayenne pepper and pour in 750ml (1¼) pints water. Season with salt and pepper and bring to the boil.

◆ Transfer the casserole dish to the oven, cover, and cook for 40–45 minutes, until the liquid is absorbed and the rice is tender. Scatter fresh coriander and chives over the pilaff and serve.

EACH SERVING CONTAINS
Kcals 400 • Protein 8g • Fat 14g (of which saturated 2g) • Carbohydrate 62g
Fibre 3g • Kcals from fat 33% • Good source of vitamins A and E

Japanese Rice Bowl with Vegetables

This is the classic Japanese way of preparing rice for sushi. It is slightly sticky and sweet with a very subtle flavour from the rice wine vinegar and dashi-konbu, a type of seaweed. The dashi-konbu adds flavour to the rice as it cooks and is available in sheets or pieces.

Serves 4
Preparation time: 20 minutes, plus 15 minutes standing time
Cooking time: 20 minutes

one 5 × 5cm (2 × 2in) piece dashi-
   konbu

225g (8oz) Japanese sushi rice

4 tablespoons rice wine vinegar

1 tablespoon caster sugar

pinch of Maldon salt

1 tablespoon vegetable oil

115g (4oz) shiitake mushrooms,
   sliced

115g (4oz) field mushrooms, sliced

2 carrots, thinly sliced

200ml (7fl oz) vegetable stock

2 tablespoons soy sauce

1 tablespoon sugar

2 teaspoons cornflour

170g (6oz) bean sprouts

150g (5½oz) sugarsnap peas

dark soy sauce, pickled ginger and
   wasabi, to serve

◆ Put the dashi-konbu and rice into a large saucepan with 450ml (15fl oz) water. Bring to the boil and remove the dashi-konbu. Cover and simmer the rice for 10 minutes. Remove from the heat.

◆ Stir 2 tablespoons vinegar and the caster sugar and salt in a small bowl until the sugar and salt have dissolved. Pour the mixture over the cooked rice. Cover and set aside for 15 minutes.

◆ Heat the oil in a wok or deep frying pan. Add the shiitake and field mushrooms and carrots and fry over a moderate heat for 5 minutes until lightly browned. Add the stock, soy sauce, remaining vinegar, sugar and cornflour. Bring to a simmer and cook gently for 5 minutes until the sauce is slightly thickened. Stir in the bean sprouts and sugarsnap peas and cook for 1 minute.

◆ Tranfer the rice to a warm serving dish. Spoon the vegetables over the rice and serve with little bowls of soy sauce, pickled ginger and wasabi as accompaniments.

EACH SERVING CONTAINS
Kcals 315 • Protein 8g • Fat 4g (of which saturated 0.5g) • Carbohydrate 64g
Fibre 5g • Kcals from fat 12% • Good source of vitamins C and A

Spring Vegetables with Saffron Basmati Rice

This is a quick main course that looks as pretty and delicious as it tastes. Despite the few ingredients the flavour is fabulous. There is something magical about saffron and the way it washes a golden hue over everything. A good way to maximize the flavour and colour of the threads is to toast them in a metal spoon over a low heat and pound them using a pestle and mortar before steeping them in a few tablespoons of warm liquid. This kind of recipe extols the virtues of fresh vegetables. If you do not appreciate vegetables that have bite, you will need to cook them for a little longer. I like to use baby vegetables, but if these are unavailable larger ones will do just as well.

Serves 4
Preparation time: 15 minutes
Cooking time: 20 minutes

350g (12¼oz) basmati rice

2 medium-sized tomatoes

large pinch of saffron threads

300ml (10fl oz) hot vegetable stock (see page 55)

2 tablespoons olive oil

8 large spring onions, cut diagonally into thin slices

400g (14oz) carrots, cut diagonally into thin slices

400g (14oz) leeks, cut diagonally into thin slices

400g (14oz) courgettes, cut diagonally into thin slices

Maldon salt and freshly ground black pepper

handful of fresh flat-leaf parsley, roughly chopped, to serve

♦ Bring a large saucepan of water to the boil and add the rice. Bring back to the boil, reduce the heat and simmer for 15–20 minutes until the rice is tender. Drain and keep warm.

♦ Meanwhile, put the tomatoes in a bowl and cover with boiling water. Leave them for exactly 20 seconds then plunge them straight into cold water. Drain and skin the tomatoes then roughly chop the flesh. Put the saffron threads in a little bowl and cover with 2 tablespoons vegetable stock. Leave to soak for 5 minutes.

♦ Heat the olive oil in a wok or deep frying pan and sauté the spring onions over a high heat for about 3 minutes until soft. Add the carrots, leeks and courgettes and cook for a further 5 minutes, stirring occasionally. You may need to use 2 spoons to toss everything together. Stir in the tomatoes, stock, saffron and its liquid and season with salt and pepper. Simmer for 3 minutes.

◆ Divide the rice between 4 warm bowls. Pile the vegetables on the rice using a slotted spoon, then drizzle their juices over the top. Scatter fresh parsley over them and serve.

EACH SERVING CONTAINS
Kcals 450 • Protein 12g • Fat 7g (of which saturated 1g) • Carbohydrate 82g • Fibre 6g
Kcals from fat 15% • Excellent source of vitamins C and A • Good source of folic acid

Spicy Vegetables and Coconut Cream

For maximum flavour, cook the spicy vegetables the night before and keep them in the fridge. Reheat gently while you cook the rice. Coconut cream is very thick and creamy. Use unsweetened coconut milk instead if you prefer, but omit the water from the recipe.

Serves 4
Preparation time: 20 minutes
Cooking time: 25 minutes

900g (2lb) mixed vegetables, such as broccoli, carrots, baby corn, tomatoes

2 tablespoons vegetable oil

1 large onion, sliced

4cm (2in) piece fresh root ginger, peeled and chopped

2 garlic cloves, crushed

1 lemon grass stick, thinly sliced

1 red chilli, seeded and finely chopped

2 teaspoons medium curry powder

200ml (7fl oz) coconut cream

large handful of fresh basil leaves, roughly torn

large handful of fresh coriander leaves, roughly chopped

340g (12oz) Thai jasmine rice

Maldon salt and freshly ground black pepper

To serve

large handful of fresh basil leaves, roughly torn

large handful of fresh coriander leaves, roughly chopped

◆ If using tomatoes, skin them (see page 41) and roughly chop their flesh. Cut the other vegetables into bite-sized pieces.

◆ Heat the oil in a large saucepan. Add the onion, ginger, garlic and lemon grass and sauté over a moderate heat for 5 minutes until softened. Stir in the chilli and curry powder and season with salt and pepper. Cook for a further 5 minutes. Add the vegetables and cook for 5 minutes, then mix in the coconut cream and 200ml (7fl oz) water. Simmer gently, covered, for 15 minutes. Mix the fresh basil and coriander into the vegetables.

◆ Stir the rice into a large saucepan of boiling water and simmer for 10–15 minutes until tender – the rice should have a little bite left in it. Drain.

◆ Divide the rice between 4 warm bowls and top with the vegetables. Scatter fresh basil and coriander over them and serve.

EACH SERVING CONTAINS
Kcals 610 • Protein 15g • Fat 20g (of which saturated 11g) • Carbohydrate 93g • Fibre 6g
Kcals from fat 30% • Excellent source of vitamins C and A • Good source of folic acid

Maize with Beans

This recipe comes all the way from Ras Kutani, a beach resort in East Africa which I found particularly stunning as I was on my honeymoon. Corn maize (or 'meal', also known as polenta) and beans is the staple local diet – not a dish that appeared on the hotel menu. However, when I expressed an interest in their food, the staff were more than delighted to cook this dish and share it with us, on one condition: that we ate it with our hands! This is easier than it may seem. Take a piece of corn maize, roll it into a ball, dip the ball into the beans and enjoy. (I must confess I used a spoon towards the end – I didn't want to waste any of the delicious juices.)

Serves 4
Preparation time: 20 minutes
Cooking time: 20 minutes

2 tablespoons sunflower oil

1 large onion, finely chopped

2 teaspoons turmeric

200ml (7fl oz) unsweetened
    coconut milk

400g (14oz) can kidney beans,
    drained

150g (5½oz) corn meal

◆ Heat the oil in a frying pan and sauté the onions over a high heat for 3 minutes or until they soften and start to go golden. Add the turmeric and cook, stirring, for a further 2 minutes. Stir in the coconut milk and bring to the boil. Add the beans and simmer for 10 minutes.

◆ Put 300ml (10fl oz) water in a large saucepan and bring to the boil. Add the corn meal by letting it run through your fingers in a thin stream while beating continuously over a moderate heat. The maize is cooked when the mixture leaves the sides of the pan.

◆ Pile the maize in a mound on a warm dish and divide the beans between 4 warm bowls. Guests can have fun taking balls of the maize and dipping them into their beans. Alternatively, spoon a little pile of maize in the centres of 4 warm plates, top with the beans and eat with a fork or spoon.

EACH SERVING CONTAINS
Kcals 350 • Protein 11g • Fat 12g (of which saturated 5g) • Carbohydrate 47g
Fibre 7g • Kcals from fat 32% • Good source of vitamin E

Juma's Special African Curry

Special thanks go to Juma Mashaka, the cook at Ras Kutani Hotel on the coast of East Africa where I sampled this dish. I have adapted it slightly and this version is one of my favourites for four reasons: it is incredibly quick to prepare; you need only a few ingredients; you can use any vegetables that you happen to have available, and, last but by no means least, it brings back fond memories of my honeymoon.

Serves 4
Preparation time: 15 minutes
Cooking time: 25 minutes

6 medium-sized tomatoes

3 tablespoons sunflower oil

2 large onions, chopped

6 garlic cloves, finely chopped

1 orange pepper, seeded and
   coarsely chopped

2 tablespoons medium Madras
   curry powder

400ml (14fl oz) can unsweetened
   coconut milk

2 teaspoons creamed coconut

4 red chillies, seeded and chopped

675g (1½lb) mixed fresh vegetables,
   such as carrots, sugarsnap
   peas, baby corn and so on

2 courgettes, sliced

grated zest of 1 large lime

300g (10½oz) basmati rice

handful of fresh coriander leaves,
   roughly chopped

handful of fresh flat-leaf parsley,
   roughly chopped

◆ Put the tomatoes in a bowl and cover with boiling water. Leave them for exactly 20 seconds then plunge them straight into cold water. Drain and skin the tomatoes then chop their flesh.

◆ Heat the oil in a large saucepan. Add the onions, garlic, orange pepper and curry powder, and cook, stirring often, for 5 minutes or until the onion has started to soften. Stir in the tomatoes, coconut milk, coconut cream and chillies. Bring to the boil, then reduce the heat and simmer gently for 15 minutes.

◆ Meanwhile, prepare the mixed vegetables according to their type: if you are using large vegetables, chop them into bite-sized pieces; leave small produce, like sugarsnap peas, whole. Add the mixed vegetables, courgettes and half the lime zest to the sauce and continue to cook for 5 minutes.

- While the curry is simmering, bring a large saucepan of water to the boil. Add the rice and cook for about 15 minutes or until the grains are tender, then drain well. Mix the remaining lime zest with the coriander and parsley.

- Divide the freshly cooked rice between 4 warm serving bowls and spoon the curry on top. Scatter the lime zest and herb mixture over the top and serve immediately.

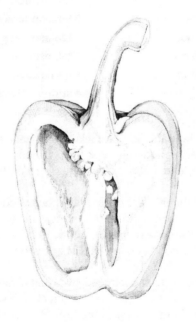

EACH SERVING CONTAINS
Kcals 330 • Protein 8g • Fat 21g (of which saturated 10g) • Carbohydrate 26g • Fibre 7g
Kcals from fat 58% • Excellent source of vitamins C, A and E

Wontons with Chilli Sauce

If you can't find fresh shiitake mushrooms for this dish, use dried porcini and soak them in warm water for 30 minutes before use. If rice wine vinegar is unavailable, use slightly less white wine vinegar instead.

Serves 4
Preparation time: 25 minutes
Cooking time: 10–12 minutes

1 tablespoon vegetable oil

115g (4oz) field mushrooms, finely chopped

75g (2½oz) shiitake mushrooms, finely chopped

2 spring onions, finely chopped

1 tablespoon soy sauce

1 tablespoon dry sherry

2 teaspoons sesame oil

pinch of sugar

pinch of salt

3–4 large lettuce leaves

1 packet (25) wonton wrappers

For the chilli sauce

4 tablespoons light soy sauce

2 tablespoons rice wine vinegar

1 tablespoon sesame oil

1 tablespoon hot chilli sauce

1 garlic clove, crushed

4 spring onions, finely chopped

♦ Heat the oil in a frying pan. Add the field and shiitake mushrooms and onions and sauté over a moderate heat for 5 minutes until softened. Add the soy sauce, sherry and sesame oil and season with the salt and sugar.

♦ Put 1 tablespoon of the mixture on the non-floured side of a wonton wrapper, moisten the edges with water and fold the wrapper over to form a little purse. Pinch the edges together tightly to close. Repeat the process until all the stuffing is used. You will probably fill about 20 wrappers.

♦ Line a heatproof plate with the lettuce leaves and arrange the wontons on top in a single layer. Put a wooden or metal rack in a wok or wide pan, pour in 5cm (2in) water and bring to the boil. Put the plate on the rack, cover and steam for 6–7 minutes or until the wontons are firm to the touch. While the wontons are cooking, put all the chilli sauce ingredients in a screw-top jar and shake vigorously until well blended.

♦ Divide the wontons between 4 warm plates and serve with the chilli sauce as an accompaniment.

EACH SERVING CONTAINS
Kcals 130 • Protein 2.5g • Fat 8.5g (of which saturated 1g) • Carbohydrate 10g
Fibre 1g • Kcals from fat 60%

Chillied Spring Rolls with a Dipping Sauce

There may seem to be a lot of chillies here but the hot seeds and membranes are removed in this recipe. Here chillies are used for their flavour. Remember to keep the filo pastry covered with a clean damp cloth when you are not working with it, to prevent it from drying out.

Makes 8 spring rolls
Preparation time: 20 minutes
Cooking time: 12–15 minutes

3 tablespoons pine nuts

8–10 green chillies

2 tablespoons vegetable oil, plus extra for brushing

2 bunches of spring onions, cut diagonally into thin slices

2 garlic cloves, chopped

1 tablespoon grated peeled fresh root ginger

225g (8oz) bean sprouts

2 teaspoons sesame oil

225g (8oz) filo pastry, thawed if frozen

For the dipping sauce

100ml (3½fl oz) soy sauce

4cm (1½in) piece fresh root ginger, peeled and finely sliced

3 garlic cloves, crushed

Preheat the oven to 180°C/350°F/Gas 4. Dry-fry the pine nuts in a heavy-based frying pan over a moderate heat, stirring frequently until golden. Seed the chillies, scraping away the membranes, and slice them finely.

Heat the oil in a wok or large frying pan. Add the spring onions, garlic, chillies and ginger and stir-fry over a high heat for 5 minutes. Add the bean sprouts and the pine nuts and stir-fry for a further 2 minutes. Add the sesame oil and toss. Remove from the heat and leave to cool.

Spread out a sheet of filo pastry and cut it in half. Cover the other half and the remaining sheets with a clean, damp cloth. Brush the pastry half with a little oil and put 1 tablespoon of the filling in the centre. Fold the sides over to enclose the filling, then roll the pastry over to form a spring roll. Brush the edges with a little oil and press them firmly together to seal. Place on a baking tray. Repeat with the remaining pastry and filling. Bake the spring rolls for 12–15 minutes until golden and crisp.

Put all the sauce ingredients in a screw-top jar and shake vigorously until well blended. Serve the spring rolls with the sauce as an accompaniment.

EACH SERVING CONTAINS
Kcals 175 • Protein 4g • Fat 10g (of which saturated 1g) • Carbohydrate 17g
Fibre 1g • Kcals from fat 53%

Sticky Golden Onion Tarts

To achieve really caramelized onions, always add any acidic liquids towards the end of cooking. The wine, vinegar and lemon juice will also help to counterbalance the sweet flavour of the onions. The Vegan Society has a list of wines that do not contain animal-derived products.

Serves 4
Preparation time: 20 minutes
Cooking time: about 1 hour

3 tablespoons olive oil

2 Spanish onions, sliced

2 leeks, cut diagonally into thin
   slices

1 red onion, cut into thin wedges

150ml (5fl oz) organic white wine

3 tablespoons white wine vinegar

1 tablespoon lemon juice

375g (13oz) puff pastry, thawed if
   frozen

Maldon salt and freshly ground
   black pepper

handful of fresh chives, finely
   chopped

◆ Preheat the oven to 190°C/375°F/Gas 5. Heat the oil in a saucepan or a frying pan with a lid. Add the Spanish onions, leeks and red onion and stir until coated with the oil. Cover and cook very slowly and gently for 1 hour. Season generously with salt and pepper. Increase the heat, add the wine, vinegar and lemon juice. Stir until the wine has almost disappeared. Remove from the heat.

◆ While the onions are cooking, roll out the pastry on a floured surface and use a saucer to cut out four 10cm (4in) circles. Prick the bases all over with a fork. When the onions have been cooking for about 40 minutes, put a baking tray in the oven for 1 minute to heat. Place the circles on the baking tray and bake for 10–15 minutes until golden and puffy. Turn the circles over, spoon some sticky caramelized onions on to each one and bake for a further 5 minutes.

◆ Put the tarts on 4 warm plates, scatter fresh chives over them and serve.

EACH SERVING CONTAINS
Kcals 495 • Protein 7g • Fat 30g (of which saturated 1g) • Carbohydrate 44g
Fibre 2.5g • Kcals from fat 56%

Tuscan Tarts

I describe these tarts as Tuscan because they are packed with the wonderful ingredients so often associated with the region's cooking: olives, tomatoes, basil and peppers. You very often need only a few ingredients with their own fresh flavours to make a recipe a success. This is a classic example. Roasted peppers are available in jars and also at supermarket delicatessen counters.

Serves 4
Preparation time: 20 minutes
Cooking time: 20 minutes

225g (8oz) ripe tomatoes
1 tablespoon olive oil
1 large onion, sliced
1 sheet puff pastry from a 425g
   (14½oz) pack, thawed if frozen
4 tablespoons good quality
   tapenade
1 jar roasted peppers, about 225g
   (8oz), drained

large handful of mixed black and
   green olives, pitted

To serve
extra virgin olive oil, for drizzling
handful of fresh flat-leaf parsley,
   finely chopped, *or* fresh basil
   leaves, roughly torn

◆ Preheat the oven to 200°C/400°F/Gas 6. Put the tomatoes in a bowl and cover with boiling water. Leave them for exactly 20 seconds then plunge them straight into cold water. Drain and peel the tomatoes then quarter them. Set aside.

◆ Heat the oil in a frying pan and sauté the onion over a moderate heat for about 5 minutes until soft and golden.

◆ Cut the pastry sheet into quarters and place them on a baking tray. Spread 1 tablespoon tapenade over the middle of each quarter, leaving a border of about 1cm (½in). Cut the peppers into strips. Combine them with the tomatoes, sautéed onion and olives and divide the mixture between the pastry quarters. Smooth it over the tapenade, making sure you don't cover the border.

◆ Bake for 15 minutes or until the pastry is golden and puffy. Drizzle a little olive oil over the top, scatter the fresh parsley or basil over the tarts and serve warm.

EACH SERVING CONTAINS
Kcals 390 • Protein 4.5g • Fat 30g (of which saturated 2.5g) • Carbohydrate 28g
Fibre 3g • Kcals from fat 65% • Good source of vitamins C and A

Griddled Vegetables on Lemon Grass Sticks with Coriander Basmati

Firm blades of aromatic lemon grass make novel, flavour-imparting skewers for these colourful griddled vegetables. Served with basmati rice tossed with coriander chutney, they make a deliciously quick meal. Of course, you can always use wooden satay sticks instead of the lemon grass and chopped fresh coriander can be mixed with the rice instead of the chutney when you are in a real hurry. When warm weather is the inspiration for al fresco cooking, grill these little kebabs on the barbecue.

Serves 4

Preparation time: 30 minutes, plus 1 hour's marinating
Cooking time: about 15 minutes

2 tablespoons groundnut oil, plus extra for brushing vegetables

3 shallots, finely sliced

3 garlic cloves, roughly chopped

2.5cm (1in) piece fresh root ginger, peeled and roughly chopped

2 tablespoons soy sauce

juice of ½ orange

grated zest and juice of ½ lime

2 tablespoons golden caster sugar

1 teaspoon turmeric

1 teaspoon ground coriander

½ teaspoon cayenne pepper

2 red peppers, seeded and cut into bite-sized chunks

1 yellow pepper, seeded and cut into bite-sized chunks

1 aubergine, cut into bite-sized chunks

2 courgettes, cut into bite-sized chunks

2 yellow courgettes or 4 patty pan, cut into bite-sized chunks

8 lemon grass sticks, or wooden satay skewers, to cook

350g (12¼oz) basmati rice

handful of fresh coriander leaves, roughly chopped, to serve

For the coriander chutney

55g (2oz) fresh coriander leaves, roughly chopped

1 tablespoon ground almonds

2.5cm (1in) piece fresh root ginger, peeled and roughly chopped

2 garlic cloves, peeled and roughly crushed

juice of ½ lime

2 red chillies, seeded and finely chopped

Maldon salt and freshly ground black pepper

♦ Heat the oil in a large frying pan or saucepan. Add and sauté the shallots, garlic and ginger over a moderate heat for a few minutes until golden.

- Stir in the soy sauce, orange juice, lime zest and juice, sugar, turmeric, ground coriander, cayenne pepper and 1 tablespoon water. Cook for a couple more minutes, then remove this marinade from the heat and leave to cool.

- Add the prepared vegetables to the marinade and toss everything together so that all the pieces are well coated. Cover and set aside to marinate for at least 1 hour.

- Meanwhile, make the coriander chutney: Mix the coriander leaves, almonds, ginger, garlic and lime juice with the chillies. Season with salt and pepper.

- Soak the lemon grass sticks or skewers in cold water for 10 minutes. Pierce a hole through the middle of each piece of vegetable and thread the pieces on to the lemon grass sticks or skewers. Divide the vegetables equally between the lemon grass, alternating the pieces as you thread them on to the grass. Set aside while you preheat the grill on the hottest setting.

- Meanwhile, bring a large saucepan of water to the boil. Add the rice and cook for about 15 minutes or until the grains are tender, then drain well.

- While the rice is cooking, brush the vegetables with groundnut oil and grill them for about 5 minutes. Baste the vegetables with any remaining marinade, turn them over and cook for another 5 minutes.

- Fork half the coriander chutney through the rice. Spoon the hot rice into 4 warm bowls or on to plates. Top each portion with a couple of vegetable skewers. Scatter fresh coriander leaves over the top and serve immediately, offering the remaining coriander chutney as an accompaniment.

EACH SERVING CONTAINS

Kcals 475 • Protein 11g • Fat 9g (of which saturated 1.5g) • Carbohydrate 86g • Fibre 4g • Kcals from fat 17% • Excellent source of vitamins B_1, niacin, B_6, folic acid, C, A and E • Good source of phosphorus

Roasted Vegetables with Couscous and Lemon Pepper Oil

Soaking the couscous as well as baking it makes the grains light and fluffy. Serve the roast garlic cloves whole so that everyone can squeeze the flesh out of the skins and enjoy the delicious flavour.

Serves 4
Preparation time: 20 minutes
Cooking time: 30 minutes

---

1 fennel bulb

12 medium-sized vine-ripened
tomatoes

2 red peppers, seeded and cut into
bite-sized chunks

2 courgettes, cut into bite-sized
chunks

1 red onion, cut into bite-sized
chunks

4 cloves garlic, unpeeled

4 tablespoons extra virgin olive oil

grated zest of 1 lemon

450g (1lb) couscous

freshly ground black pepper

To serve

large handful of fresh coriander
leaves, roughly chopped

4 lemon wedges

◆ Preheat the oven to 200°C/400°F/Gas 6. Trim the tough stalks off the fennel bulb, shave off the base and remove any damaged outer layers. Slice the bulb in half lengthways, cut out the core and slice each half into bite-sized chunks. Skin the tomatoes (see page 41), then cut them into bite-sized chunks.

◆ Put the fennel, tomatoes, peppers, courgettes, onion and garlic in an ovenproof dish. Drizzle 2–3 tablespoons oil over them and scatter pepper and half the lemon zest over the top. Bake for 30 minutes until slightly golden around the edges.

◆ Put the couscous in another ovenproof dish and pour warm water over the top – just enough to cover the grains and not flood them. Cover and leave for at least 10 minutes in a warm place. Fluff up the couscous grains with a fork. Add the remaining oil and lemon zest and mix together. Cover the couscous with foil, bake alongside the vegetables for 20 minutes.

◆ Mix the couscous and vegetables together and scatter fresh coriander over them. Serve warm with lemon wedges and extra black pepper.

EACH SERVING CONTAINS
Kcals 425 • Protein 9g • Fat 13g (of which saturated 2g) • Carbohydrate 70g • Fibre 4.5g
Kcals from fat 25% • Excellent source of vitamins C and A • Good source of vitamin E

Malaysian Vegetables

Cooking cannot get simpler than this. This dish is quick to prepare and takes ten minutes to cook. To make the meal complete, serve the vegetables with a bread of your choice or a bowl of freshly steamed rice.

Serves 4
Preparation time: 10 minutes
Cooking time: 10 minutes

---

5 plum tomatoes
2 tablespoons vegetable oil
1 Spanish onion, finely sliced
2 garlic cloves, finely chopped
125g (4½oz) mangetout
125g (4½oz) frozen peas
6 baby carrots, quartered
1 teaspoon turmeric
1 teaspoon chilli powder

400ml (14fl oz) can unsweetened
coconut milk
225g (8oz) Chinese cabbage, thinly
sliced
Maldon salt and freshly ground
black pepper
handful of fresh coriander leaves,
roughly chopped, to serve

◆ Put the tomatoes in a bowl and cover with boiling water. Leave them for exactly 20 seconds then plunge them straight into cold water. Drain and skin the tomatoes then cut them into bite-sized chunks.

◆ Heat the oil in a wok or large frying pan. Add the onion and garlic and sauté over a moderate heat for 5 minutes or until softened. Add the mangetout, peas, carrots, turmeric, chilli powder and coconut milk. Simmer for 3 minutes, stirring constantly. Add the sliced cabbage and tomato chunks and simmer, stirring, for a further 3 minutes. Season with salt and pepper.

◆ Divide the vegetables between 4 warm plates, scatter fresh coriander over them and serve.

EACH SERVING CONTAINS
Kcals 235 • Protein 5g • Fat 16g (of which saturated 10g) • Carbohydrate 14g • Fibre 5g
Kcals from fat 64% • Excellent source of vitamins C and A • Good source of folic acid and vitamin B_1

Mediterranean Potatoes with Olives, Herbs and Tomatoes

These potatoes are visually appealing and very satisfying. All they need to accompany them is a fresh green salad dressed in a vinaigrette. The many new and exciting ingredients on the market today make life as a food writer very interesting indeed. Sun blush tomatoes with their pleasing garlic flavour are a good example – if you cannot find any, the sun-dried variety will work well, but you may like to add an extra clove of chopped garlic to the potatoes.

Serves 4
Preparation time: 15 minutes
Cooking time: 55 minutes

900g (2lb) waxy potatoes, unpeeled

2 tablespoons olive oil

1 Spanish onion, finely sliced

200g (7oz) sun blush tomatoes, cut into strips

200g (7oz) mixed black and green olives, pitted

450ml (15fl oz) vegetable stock (see page 55)

Maldon salt and freshly ground black pepper

large handful of fresh flat-leaf parsley, roughly chopped

◆ Preheat the oven to 190°C/375°F/Gas 5. Bring a large saucepan of water to the boil, add the potatoes and simmer for 10 minutes until they are partly cooked – they should still be firm when pierced with a sharp knife. Drain.

◆ Heat the oil in a frying pan and sauté the onion over a moderate heat for about 5 minutes until soft and golden. Peel and thinly slice the potatoes. Oil an ovenproof dish. Arrange a layer of the sliced potatoes on the bottom and season with salt and pepper. Scatter some of the onion slices, tomato strips and olives over them and season well. Arrange another layer of potato slices, then another layer of onions, tomatoes and olives. Continue the process until all the ingredients have been used, finishing with a layer of potatoes. Remember to season each layer.

◆ Bring the stock to the boil and pour it over the vegetables. Bake in the oven for 30–40 minutes until the potatoes are cooked and crispy. Scatter fresh parsley over the top and serve.

EACH SERVING CONTAINS
Kcals 300 • Protein 6g • Fat 12g (of which saturated 2g) • Carbohydrate 43g • Fibre 5g
Excellent source of vitamin C • Good source of vitamins B_1 (thiamine), B_6

Potato Cakes with Peach and Lemon Grass Chutney

There is something simply divine about these hot potato cakes served with a peach and lemon grass chutney. You will probably only use half the chutney with the cakes, so put the remainder in an airtight jar. It will keep for a few days in the fridge. If time is short, serve the potato cakes with a bought chutney of your choice. Alternatively, you could plan ahead and make the chutney when you have the time. Allow it to cool after cooking, and pour it into hot sterilized jars. Seal and store in a dark, cool place. Refrigerate once a jar has been opened.

Serves 4
Preparation time: 30 minutes
Cooking time: 40 minutes, plus chilling time for the potato cakes; 1½ hours for the chutney

---

750g (1lb 10oz) potatoes, peeled

about 2 tablespoons extra virgin olive oil

2 tablespoons vegetable oil

1 red chilli, seeded and finely sliced

1 large bunch of spring onions, finely sliced

large handful of coriander leaves, roughly chopped

4 slices white bread, crumbed

2 tablespoons paprika

Maldon salt and freshly ground black pepper

vegetable oil, for shallow frying

For the chutney

2 teaspoons sunflower oil

3 lemon grass sticks, roughly chopped

2.5cm (1in) piece fresh root ginger, peeled and roughly chopped

2 large onions, roughly chopped

2 red chillies, seeded and chopped

2 teaspoons ground coriander

900g (2lb) peaches, peeled, stoned and sliced

500ml (17fl oz) white wine vinegar

150g (5½oz) soft brown sugar

125g (4½oz) currants

handful of fresh coriander leaves, roughly chopped

- ◆ Make the chutney: Heat the oil in a saucepan. Add the lemon grass, ginger, onions, chillies and ground coriander and cook over a moderate heat for 2 minutes. Reduce the heat to low. Add the peaches, vinegar, sugar and currants. Stir the mixture until the sugar has dissolved. Increase the temperature and simmer gently for 1½ hours, stirring occasionally, until the mixture is thick. Leave to cool. Add the coriander leaves and mix well.

▶

◆ Preheat the oven to 150°C/300°F/Gas 2. Line a plate or baking tray with kitchen paper. Make the potato cakes: Put the potatoes in a large saucepan of boiling water and simmer for about 15 minutes until tender. Drain. Return the potatoes to the saucepan and dry them out over a low heat, shaking the pan gently. Mash the potato with about 1 tablespoon olive oil and season well with salt and pepper.

◆ Heat the vegetable oil in a wok or large frying pan and sauté the chilli and spring onions over a moderate heat for 5 minutes or until soft. Spoon the spring onions on to the mashed potato. Add the coriander leaves and mix well. Cover and chill for 30 minutes.

◆ Shape the potato mixture into rounds and brush with a little oil. Mix the breadcrumbs with the paprika and spread them out on a plate. Dip the potato cakes into the crumbs, turning and pressing them gently so that they are coated all over.

◆ Heat a thin layer of vegetable oil in a frying pan and fry the potato cakes in batches over a moderate heat for about 5 minutes until golden all over. Drain the batches on the kitchen paper and keep warm in the oven. Divide the potato cakes between 4 warm plates and serve with big spoonfuls of peach and lemon grass chutney.

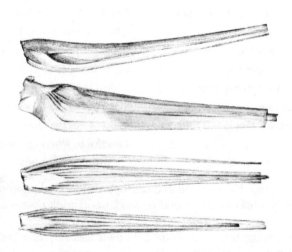

EACH SERVING CONTAINS
Kcals 645 • Protein 11g • Fat 13g (of which saturated 2g) • Carbohydrate 129g
Fibre 7.5g • Kcals from fat 19% • Good source of vitamins C and E

Moroccan Spiced Red Potato with Chick Peas

This very satisfying dish can quite happily be served on its own. However, it is also delicious on a bed of steamed couscous as the little grains absorb some of the Moroccan-flavoured juices.

Serves 4
Preparation time: 20 minutes
Cooking time: 40 minutes

2 red-skinned potatoes, unpeeled

450g (1lb) fresh ripe plum tomatoes
  or a 400g (14oz) can chopped
  tomatoes

1 teaspoon cumin seeds

2 tablespoons olive oil

1 large onion, chopped

1 large garlic clove, chopped

large pinch of saffron threads

4cm (2in) piece fresh root ginger,
  peeled and chopped

415g (14½oz) can chick peas,
  drained

1–2 teaspoons harissa

Maldon salt and freshly ground
  black pepper

handful of fresh coriander leaves,
  roughly chopped

handful of fresh mint leaves,
  roughly chopped

◆ Put the potatoes in a small saucepan of boiling water and simmer for about 20 minutes until tender. Drain and leave to cool. Cut the potatoes into cubes, leaving the skins on. Set aside. If you are using fresh tomatoes, skin them (see page 41) and roughly chop their flesh.

◆ Dry-fry the cumin seeds in a heavy-based frying pan over a moderate heat, turning or stirring frequently, for a couple of minutes until they start to pop and turn golden. Crush coarsely using a pestle and mortar.

◆ Heat the oil in a large saucepan. Add the onion, garlic, saffron, ginger and cumin and sauté over a moderate heat for 5 minutes until the onion is soft and golden. Stir in the tomatoes, diced potatoes, chick peas and harissa and pour in 180ml (6fl oz) water. Bring to the boil then reduce the heat and simmer, covered, for 20 minutes. Season with salt and pepper.

◆ Transfer the potatoes to a warm serving dish, scatter fresh coriander and mint over them and serve.

EACH SERVING CONTAINS
Kcals 270 • Protein 10g • Fat 9g (of which saturated 1g) • Carbohydrate 39g
Fibre 7g • Kcals from fat 30% • Good source of vitamins C and E

Indian Vegetables

I must confess that when I ate this dish it was made with ghee (clarified butter). However, I was equally pleased with the end result when I developed a version using oil. As always, I have toasted the cumin seeds before crushing them to bring out their full flavour.

Serves 4
Preparation time: 20 minutes
Cooking time: 25 minutes

1 teaspoon cumin seeds

200g (7oz) plum tomatoes *or*
  canned tomatoes

350g (12¼oz) basmati rice

1 tablespoon vegetable oil

1 large onion, sliced

3 garlic cloves, finely chopped

1 teaspoon turmeric

4 carrots, finely sliced

6 okra, halved lengthways

¼ cabbage, shredded

125g (4½oz) green beans, trimmed

2 green chillies, seeded and
  chopped

2.5cm (1in) piece fresh root ginger,
  peeled and grated

handful of fresh coriander, roughly
  chopped, to serve

◆ Dry-fry the cumin seeds in a heavy-based frying pan over a moderate heat, turning or stirring frequently, for a couple of minutes until they start to pop and turn golden. Crush coarsely using a pestle and mortar.

◆ If you are using fresh plum tomatoes, put them in a bowl and cover with boiling water. Leave them for exactly 20 seconds then plunge them straight into cold water. Drain and skin the tomatoes then roughly chop their flesh.

◆ Bring a large saucepan of water to the boil and add the rice. Bring back to the boil, reduce the heat and simmer for 15–20 minutes until the rice is tender. Drain.

◆ Meanwhile, heat the oil in a large frying pan and sauté the onion over a moderate heat for about 5 minutes or until brown. Add the garlic, cumin seeds and turmeric and fry, stirring, for a further 2 minutes. Reduce the heat to low. Add the carrots, okra, cabbage and green beans and cook, stirring, for a further 5 minutes. Stir in the tomatoes, chillies and ginger. Cover and simmer for 10 minutes. The vegetables should be just tender. Scatter fresh coriander over them and serve with the fluffy basmati rice.

EACH SERVING CONTAINS
Kcals 424 • Protein 11g • Fat 4.5g (of which saturated 0.5g) • Carbohydrate 84g • Fibre 7g
Kcals from fat 10% • Excellent source of vitamins C and A • Good source of folic acid

Balti

I used to live in Henley-in-Arden, near to the balti land of Birmingham, and it was there that I learnt the basics of balti. As with all cooking, it is amazing what a difference it makes if you use whole spices and dry-fry them to bring out their flavour. Serve this balti with warm naan bread to mop up the juices.

Serves 4
Preparation time: 15 minutes
Cooking time: 10–12 minutes

5 medium-sized vine-ripened tomatoes; choose ripe, juicy ones

1 teaspoon coriander seeds

½ teaspoon cumin seeds

½ teaspoon fennel seeds

6 whole green cardamoms

2 teaspoons fenugreek leaves

½ teaspoon freshly ground black pepper

½ teaspoon turmeric

3 tablespoons vegetable oil

½ cinnamon stick

3 garlic cloves, finely chopped

1 large onion, finely sliced

2 green chillies, seeded and sliced into rings

1 red pepper, seeded and roughly chopped

1 yellow pepper, seeded and roughly chopped

150g (5½oz) field mushrooms, sliced

400g (14oz) fresh spinach leaves

400g (14oz) can chick peas, drained; reserve half the liquid

1 tablespoon mango chutney

Maldon salt and freshly ground black pepper

To serve

½ handful of fresh mint leaves, roughly chopped

½ handful of fresh coriander leaves, roughly chopped

◆ Put the tomatoes in a bowl and cover with boiling water. Leave them for exactly 20 seconds then plunge them straight into cold water. Drain and skin the tomatoes then roughly chop their flesh.

◆ Dry-fry the coriander, cumin and fennel seeds, cardamom and fenugreek leaves in a heavy-based frying pan over a moderate heat, turning or stirring frequently, for about 1 minute. Leave to cool, then crush coarsely using a pestle and mortar. Add the pepper and turmeric and mix well.

▶

- Heat the oil in a wok or large frying pan. Add the spice mixture, cinnamon stick, garlic and onion and fry over a moderate heat for 5 minutes, stirring constantly. Increase the heat, add the chillies, red and yellow peppers and mushrooms and stir-fry for 3 minutes. Add the spinach and tomatoes and stir-fry for a further 3 minutes. Add the chick peas and their reserved liquid and the mango chutney. Add more water if the vegetables seem to be drying out. Stir-fry for 2–3 minutes then season with salt and pepper.

- Divide the balti between 4 warm plates, scatter fresh mint and coriander over the top and serve.

EACH SERVING CONTAINS
Kcals 285 • Protein 13g • Fat 13g (of which saturated 1.5g) • Carbohydrate 31g • Fibre 9g
Kcals from fat 41% • Excellent source of vitamins C, A and E • Good source of folic acid

Stir-Fried Black Beans with Lime and Chilli

Warm tortillas can hold many fillings and are always great fun to serve to friends. Provide a pile of warm tortillas, a bowl of hot beans and a dish of lime chunks, then leave everyone to help themselves.

Serves 4
Preparation time: 15 minutes
Cooking time: 20 minutes

8 tortillas

1 teaspoon cumin seeds

1 tablespoon vegetable oil

2 red onions, sliced into rings

2 garlic cloves, thinly sliced

1 teaspoon ground coriander

½–1 teaspoon chilli powder, preferably Kashmiri chilli powder

150ml (5fl oz) vegetable stock (see page 55)

two 415g (14½oz) cans black beans, drained

juice of ½ lime

Maldon salt and freshly ground black pepper

To serve

large handful of fresh coriander leaves, roughly chopped

4 wedges fresh lime

◆ Preheat the oven to 160°C/325°F/Gas 3. Wrap the tortillas in aluminium foil and warm them through in the oven for 10 minutes.

◆ Dry-fry the cumin seeds in a heavy-based frying pan over a moderate heat, turning or stirring frequently, for a couple of minutes until the seeds start to pop and turn golden. Crush coarsely using a pestle and mortar.

◆ Heat the oil in a wok or large frying pan and sauté the onions over a moderate heat for 5 minutes until soft and starting to turn golden. Add the garlic, ground coriander, crushed cumin and chilli powder and cook, stirring, for a further 3 minutes. Pour in the stock and simmer for about 10 minutes until the liquid is reduced by half. Add the beans and heat them through. Stir in the lime juice and season with salt and pepper.

◆ Divide the beans between 4 warm bowls and scatter fresh coriander over them. Serve with the warm tortillas and wedges of lime.

EACH SERVING CONTAINS
Kcals 540 • Protein 23g • Fat 5g (of which saturated 0.5g) • Carbohydrate 105g
Fibre 16g • Kcals from fat 9% • Good source of vitamin B$_1$ (thiamine)

Thai Green Vegetable Curry

You will only need 2 tablespoons of curry paste for this dish, but the paste will keep for a week in the fridge so you can use it for other dishes like Thai Pumpkin and Coconut Soup (see page 47).

Serves 4
Preparation time: 20 minutes
Cooking time: 15 minutes

225g (8oz) Thai jasmine rice

a 400ml (14fl oz) can unsweetened coconut milk

200ml (7fl oz) vegetable stock (see page 55)

2 tablespoons Thai curry paste

pinch of Maldon salt

5 kaffir lime leaves

225g (8oz) sugarsnap peas, halved lengthways

225g (8oz) baby corn, halved lengthways

225g (8oz) petits pois

1 red pepper, seeded and thinly sliced

1 orange pepper, seeded and thinly sliced

handful of fresh basil leaves, roughly torn, to serve

For the Thai curry paste

5 green chilli peppers, seeded and roughly chopped

1½ lemon grass sticks, thinly sliced

2 tablespoons roughly chopped fresh coriander leaves

1 teaspoon cumin seeds

2.5cm (1in) piece fresh root ginger, peeled and roughly chopped

3 spring onions, roughly chopped

2 garlic cloves, roughly chopped

1 teaspoon black peppercorns

½ teaspoon ground cinnamon

grated zest and juice of ½ lime

◆ Make the Thai curry paste: Put all the ingredients in a food processor and process until smooth. Set aside.

◆ Stir the rice into a large saucepan of boiling water and simmer for 10–15 minutes until cooked – the rice should have a little bite left in it. Drain.

◆ Meanwhile, bring the coconut milk to the boil in another saucepan. Stir in 2 tablespoons Thai curry paste (store the remainder in a screw-top jar) and add the salt and lime leaves. Add the sugarsnap peas, baby corn, petits pois and red and orange peppers and simmer, covered, for 10 minutes. Spoon the light fluffy rice into 4 warm serving bowls. Spoon the vegetable curry on to the rice, scatter fresh basil over the top and serve.

EACH SERVING CONTAINS
Kcals 405 • Protein 12g • Fat 11g (of which saturated 9g) • Carbohydrate 60g • Fibre 6.5g
Kcals from fat 26% • Excellent source of vitamins C and A

Aubergine Slices with Lemon and Fresh Coriander

Whenever I eat this I seem to end up with aubergine and lemon juices dribbling down my chin. It is a meal in itself when served with fresh bread to mop up the juices.

Serves 4
Preparation time: 10 minutes
Cooking time: 40 minutes

---

3 large aubergines

4 garlic cloves, unpeeled

5 tablespoons extra virgin olive oil

freshly ground black pepper

2 lemons, cut into chunks

To serve

large handful of fresh coriander leaves, roughly chopped

◆ Preheat the oven to 200°C/400°F/Gas 6. Slice each aubergine in half lengthways, then slice each half widthways. Make half a dozen deep diagonal slashes across each flat side, almost, but not quite, cutting through to the skin. Repeat at the opposite angle, to give a diamond effect. This will allow the heat to penetrate and the aubergines will cook more quickly.

◆ Put the aubergine halves skin-side down in a roasting tin. Add the garlic and drizzle 3 tablespoons olive oil over the top. Bake for 40 minutes until the aubergines are soft to the touch but still retain their shape.

◆ Drizzle the remaining olive oil over the aubergines and scatter fresh coriander on top. Serve warm with lots of freshly ground black pepper and chunks of lemon for squeezing.

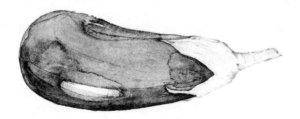

EACH SERVING CONTAINS
Kcals 160 • Protein 2g • Fat 14g (of which saturated 2g) • Carbohydrate 5g
Fibre 4.5g • Kcals from fat 84%

Aubergine Butter with Sea Salt Crusted Potatoes

This thick, chunky purée is packed with flavour and is incredibly filling. It can also be served on top of jacket potatoes or with thick fresh bread and a green salad.

Serves 4
Preparation time: 15 minutes
Cooking time: about 1 hour

4 medium-sized aubergines	2 teaspoons cumin seeds
6 fat garlic cloves	3 tablespoons tahini
6 tablespoons extra virgin olive oil	juice of 1 lime
4 large floury potatoes	large handful of fresh coriander
Maldon salt for the potatoes, plus	leaves, roughly chopped
extra for seasoning	freshly ground black pepper

◆ Preheat the oven to 225°C/425° F/Gas 7. Put the whole aubergines and garlic cloves on a baking tray. Coat the aubergines and garlic with 2 tablespoons olive oil.

◆ Put the potatoes on another baking tray. Coat them with 2 tablespoons olive oil and scatter salt to taste over them.

◆ Put both baking trays in the oven and bake for about 50 minutes until the aubergines have softened and collapsed. Remove the aubergines from the oven. Bake the potatoes for a further 10–15 minutes, depending on their size. When the aubergines have cooled a little peel them and the garlic and put the flesh in a sieve to finish cooling.

◆ Dry-fry the cumin seeds in a heavy-based frying pan over a moderate heat, turning or stirring frequently, for a couple of minutes until they start to pop and turn golden. Crush coarsely using a pestle and mortar.

◆ Put the aubergines and garlic, cumin, tahini, lime juice and remaining olive oil in a food processor and process to a purée. Put the purée in a bowl, mix in half the fresh coriander and season to taste with salt and pepper. Halve the potatoes lengthways and spoon some aubergine butter on to each half. Scatter the remaining fresh coriander over the top and serve.

EACH SERVING CONTAINS
Kcals 450 • Protein 10g • Fat 25g (of which saturated 3.5g) • Carbohydrate 50g • Fibre 10g
Kcals from fat 50% • Excellent source of vitamin C • Good source of folic acid, vitamins B_1 and B_6

Aubergine and Potato Bake

The aubergine's perfect, blemish-free purple skin never ceases to amaze me – the vegetable always looks soft, glossy and perfect. The actual flavour of its flesh could be described as rather bland but, to me, that adds to its versatility. The soft flesh will absorb spices, chillies and garlic and, similarly, can cope with strongly flavoured ingredients like chopped gherkins, olives and fresh herbs. Serve this with fresh bread.

Serves 4
Preparation time: 25 minutes
Cooking time: 50–55 minutes

900g (2lb) potatoes, peeled and cut into chunks

2 tablespoons extra virgin olive oil, plus extra for griddling and drizzling

3 large garlic cloves, crushed

450g (1lb) ripe plum tomatoes

1 large aubergine, cut into thick slices

Maldon salt and freshly ground black pepper

◆ Preheat the oven to 200°C/400°F/Gas 6. Bring a pan of water to the boil, add the potatoes, bring back to the boil and simmer for 15–20 minutes until tender. Drain, return the potatoes to the pan and dry them out over a low heat, shaking the pan gently. Add 2 tablespoons oil and the garlic and season well. Mash to a smooth purée.

◆ Put the tomatoes in a bowl and cover with boiling water. Leave them for exactly 20 seconds then plunge them straight into cold water. Drain, skin and seed the tomatoes then roughly chop the flesh.

◆ Brush a griddle pan with a little olive oil and heat until very hot. Put a few aubergine slices on the griddle and cook for 5 minutes on each side until golden and soft. Transfer them to a shallow ovenproof serving dish. Repeat with the remaining aubergine slices. If you don't have a griddle pan, put the slices into the ovenproof dish and cook in the oven for 10 minutes on each side.

◆ Spread the tomatoes over the aubergines, then spread the mashed potatoes over the tomatoes. Drizzle a little olive oil over the potatoes and scatter salt and pepper over the top. Bake for 20–25 minutes until golden and crispy and hot all the way through. Serve immediately.

EACH SERVING CONTAINS
Kcals 273 • Protein 6g • Fat 9g (of which saturated 1.5g) • Carbohydrate 43g • Fibre 5.5g
Kcals from fat 30% • Excellent source of vitamin C • Good source of vitamins B1, folic acid

Crispy Polenta Peppers and Courgettes with Balsamic Vinegar

I enjoyed something similar to this in a restaurant and had a go at making it as soon as I got home. Here is my version. It really is a nice way of serving crunchy vegetables. Don't worry if the polenta falls off the vegetables when you fry them – just serve any excess crumbs with the vegetables. Remember to cut all the vegetables into similar-sized strips so that they cook evenly. Serve them with Chunky Tomato Chutney (see page 143) for dipping and a fresh green salad tossed in a light vinaigrette.

Serves 4
Preparation time: 20 minutes, plus marinating time
Cooking time: 20 minutes

---

2 red peppers, seeded and cut into thick strips

2 orange peppers, seeded and cut into thick strips

2 courgettes, cut into thick strips

2 carrots, cut into thick strips

2 garlic cloves, crushed

2 tablespoons extra virgin olive oil

1 tablespoon balsamic vinegar

5 tablespoons fine polenta

pinch of paprika

Maldon salt and freshly ground black pepper

vegetable oil, for frying

◆ Put the peppers, courgettes, carrots and garlic in a bowl and drizzle the olive oil and vinegar over them. Leave to marinate for at least 30 minutes, stirring occasionally. Drain. Discard the marinade.

◆ Preheat the oven to 150°C/300°F/Gas 2. Line a plate or baking tray with kitchen paper. Mix the polenta and paprika in a bowl and season lightly with salt and pepper. Heat 5mm (¼in) oil in a frying pan. Toss the vegetable strips in the polenta and fry them in batches for 3–4 minutes until golden and crispy. Drain each batch on the kitchen paper and keep warm in the oven. Scoop out any excess polenta with a slotted spoon and sprinkle the crumbs over the vegetables. Serve in a warm bowl.

EACH SERVING CONTAINS
Kcals 330 • Protein 4g • Fat 20g (of which saturated 3g) • Carbohydrate 24g • Fibre 4g
Kcals from fat 65% • Excellent source of vitamins C and A

Pacific Rim Coconut Curry

This is a filling little number, perfect to serve to burly young men. I speak from experience. My brother and his friends adore this curry and don't complain of being hungry when they've eaten it – which is often the case, even when I serve them meat. I use bought pastes very rarely as I always think it pays to whizz fresh ingredients in a food processor and make my own base to a curry. So for a taste of flavours from the Pacific Rim – fresh root ginger, chilli and garlic – get your food processor out and start whizzing. Serve the curry with rice or chunks of fresh bread.

Serves 4
Preparation time: 20 minutes
Cooking time: 50 minutes

handful of coconut shavings *or* desiccated coconut

4 medium-sized vine-ripened tomatoes

3 tablespoons olive oil

2 large aubergines, about 675g (1½lb) total, cut into large chunks

1 large onion, sliced

350g (12¼oz) potatoes, peeled and diced

400ml (14fl oz) can unsweetened coconut milk

2 kaffir lime leaves *or* juice of 1 lime

300ml (10fl oz) boiling water

For the paste

30g (1oz) fresh coriander leaves

2 garlic cloves, finely chopped

2.5cm (1in) piece fresh root ginger, peeled and finely chopped

1 red chilli, seeded and finely chopped

1 green chilli, seeded and finely chopped

1 teaspoon soft brown sugar

1 tablespoon olive oil

2 tablespoons water

Maldon salt and freshly ground black pepper

♦ Make the paste: Put all the ingredients except the salt and pepper in a food processor and process until smooth. Put in a bowl and season with salt and pepper. Set aside.

♦ Dry-fry the coconut shavings or desiccated coconut in a heavy-based frying pan over a moderate heat, turning or stirring frequently, for a couple of minutes until golden. Set aside.

▶

◆ Put the tomatoes in a bowl and cover with boiling water. Leave them for exactly 20 seconds then plunge them straight into cold water. Drain and skin the tomatoes then roughly chop their flesh.

◆ Heat the olive oil in a wok or large frying pan, and fry the aubergines over a high heat for about 10 minutes until the chunks are brown all over. Don't panic – the chunks will soak up all the oil at first but as they begin to brown they will start to release it. Add the onion and fry for 2 minutes, then add the paste. Reduce the heat and fry gently for 10 minutes, stirring occasionally to prevent the vegetables sticking to the bottom of the pan.

◆ Meanwhile, add the potatoes, coconut milk, lime leaves or lime juice and boiling water to the curry. Simmer, covered, for 25 minutes. Stir occasionally to prevent the curry from sticking. Add the tomatoes a couple of minutes before the end of cooking and heat through for 1 minute.

◆ Put the curry in a warm serving bowl, scatter the toasted coconut shavings or desiccated coconut over the top and serve.

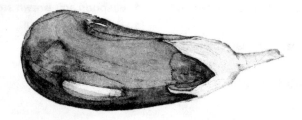

EACH SERVING CONTAINS
Kcals 325 • Protein 4.5g • Fat 22g (of which saturated 11g) • Carbohydrate 26g
Fibre 6g • Kcals from fat 61% • Excellent source of vitamin C

Roasted Red Onions and Wilted Spinach with Sweet Potatoes

I am a fan of roasting or caramelizing onions. Their natural sugars turn into a golden caramel which is sweet, sticky and simply gorgeous. In this recipe the dressing of balsamic vinegar cuts through the sweet onions and potatoes.

Serves 4
Preparation time: 20 minutes
Cooking time: 1¼ hours

---

3 red onions, peeled and cut into
   thin wedges
150ml (5fl oz) extra virgin olive oil
100ml (3½fl oz) balsamic vinegar
4 large sweet potatoes

olive oil, for frying
200g (7oz) baby spinach leaves
Maldon salt and freshly ground
   black pepper
balsamic vinegar, for drizzling

◆ Preheat the oven to 225°C/425°F/Gas 7. Put the onions into an ovenproof dish and drizzle the olive oil and vinegar over them. Season with salt and pepper. Cover the dish tightly with a lid or aluminium foil. Pierce each potato a couple of times with a skewer. Put the onions and potatoes in the oven and bake for 1 hour. Remove the potatoes. Remove the foil or lid from the onions and bake for a further 15 minutes.

◆ Heat a little olive oil in a wok or large frying pan. Add the spinach and cook over high heat for a couple of minutes until wilted. Halve the potatoes lengthways. Mix the spinach into the onions, divide the mixture between the potato halves and season well with salt and pepper. Drizzle balsamic vinegar over the top and serve.

EACH SERVING CONTAINS
Kcals 500 • Protein 5g • Fat 28g (of which saturated 4g) • Carbohydrate 59g
Fibre 8g • Kcals from fat 52% • Excellent source of vitamins C, A and E

Individual Crispy Porcini Bakes

If you are fortunate enough to have access to fresh porcini mushrooms, use them – they are a real joy. Admittedly they fetch a premium price but the consolation is that a little goes a long way. However, porcini are among the wild mushrooms that dry well. Others worth trying are morels or shiitake. To make sure you get maximum flavour (and your money's worth), use the soaking liquor in a wonderful stock for soup, the base to a stew or, as in this recipe, a sauce for pasta.

Serves 4
Preparation time: 20 minutes, plus 30 minutes standing time
Cooking time: 25 minutes

30g (1oz) dried porcini

2 tablespoons olive oil, plus extra
   for drizzling

5 shallots, sliced

4 garlic cloves, chopped

450g (1lb) field mushrooms, sliced

340g (12oz) penne pasta

55g (2oz) fresh breadcrumbs

30g (1oz) pine nuts

handful of fresh thyme leaves,
   roughly chopped

Maldon salt and freshly ground
   black pepper

◆ Pour 150ml (5fl oz) hot water over the porcini and leave to stand for 30 minutes. Drain and finely chop the porcini. Squeeze out their juice with your hands and reserve all the liquor.

◆ Heat the olive oil in a frying pan. Add the shallots and garlic and sauté over a moderate heat for a few minutes until softened and golden. They must not brown. Add the field mushrooms and cook for a further 5 minutes. Stir in the porcini and their reserved liquor and boil rapidly for 5 minutes until syrupy.

◆ Bring a large saucepan of water to the boil and cook the pasta according to the instructions on the packet. Drain and return the pasta to the saucepan. Add the mushrooms and toss well. Divide the pasta between 4 individual gratin dishes.

◆ Turn the grill to high. Spread the breadcrumbs and pine nuts out on a baking tray and toast for about 2 minutes. Mix with the thyme and scatter the mixture over the pasta. Drizzle a little olive oil on top and pop the dishes under the grill until the topping is golden. Serve immediately.

EACH SERVING CONTAINS
Kcals 480 • Protein 17g • Fat 13g (of which saturated 1g) • Carbohydrate 78g
Fibre 5g • Kcals from fat 25%

Spicy Vegetable Rounds with Chunky Tomato Chutney

Hand-held food is easy to eat and there is always an element of fun associated with it. This recipe is for those times when you feel like something hot and nourishing, on the run. The vegetable rounds can be prepared ahead of time and kept in the fridge, awaiting a quick shallow fry. (If time allows, you could bake them in a hot oven for 20 minutes.) The best way to serve them is hot inside slices of fresh ciabatta, with plenty of the chunky tomato chutney between the bread and vegetables. Supply napkins – eating can get messy.

Makes 12 vegetable rounds
Preparation time: 20 minutes
Cooking time: about 45 minutes

450g (1lb) courgettes

375g (13oz) sweet potatoes, peeled and cut into chunks

300g (10½oz) carrots, grated

1 green chilli, seeded and finely chopped

1 spring onion, thinly sliced

2 pinches of cayenne pepper, plus extra to serve

plain flour, for coating

vegetable oil, for frying

Maldon salt and freshly ground black pepper

For the chunky tomato chutney

3 medium-sized ripe tomatoes

1 tablespoon olive oil

2 shallots, thinly sliced

2 garlic cloves, crushed

2 tablespoons balsamic vinegar

1 tablespoon sugar

Maldon salt and freshly ground black pepper

handful of fresh basil leaves, roughly torn

◆ Preheat the oven to 150°C/300°F/Gas 2. Line a plate or baking tray with kitchen paper. Grate the courgettes and sprinkle with salt. Set aside for 30 minutes to draw out some of the juices, then pat dry.

◆ Make the chutney: Put the tomatoes in a bowl and cover with boiling water. Leave them for exactly 20 seconds then plunge them straight into cold water. Drain and skin the tomatoes then dice their flesh.

◆ Heat the oil in a frying pan and gently fry the shallots for about 5 minutes until softened and golden. Add the tomatoes and garlic. Raise the heat slightly and cook for a few minutes until the tomatoes have released some of their juices. Stir in the vinegar and sugar and season to taste with salt

▶

and pepper. Simmer, stirring frequently, for 3–4 minutes until the tomatoes have softened and the liquid has reduced slightly. Remove from the heat and set aside. When the chutney has cooled slightly stir in the basil leaves.

◆ Bring a saucepan of water to the boil, add the potatoes and simmer for about 15 minutes until tender. Drain, return the saucepan to the heat and dry the potatoes over a very low heat, shaking gently, then mash them. In a large bowl, mix the potato mash with the courgettes, carrots, chilli and spring onion. Add a pinch of cayenne pepper and season with salt and pepper. Using floured hands, shape the mixture into small balls. Flatten the balls slightly and coat them very lightly with flour and sprinkle with a pinch of cayenne pepper.

◆ Heat a 1cm (½in) layer of oil in a heavy-based frying pan and fry 4 vegetable rounds over a moderate to high heat for about 4 minutes on each side until golden. Drain on the kitchen paper and keep warm in the oven. Repeat the process with the remaining rounds.

◆ Sprinkle a little cayenne pepper over the vegetable rounds and serve immediately with the tomato chutney as an accompaniment.

EACH SERVING CONTAINS
Kcals 320 • Protein 4.5g • Fat 20.5g (of which saturated 2.5g) • Carbohydrate 31g
Fibre 6g • Kcals from fat 58% • Good source of vitamins C, A and E

Moroccan-Style Chick Peas with Saffron Rice

I have always been attracted to Moroccan flavours – the combination of saffron, cinnamon and ginger is just exquisite. This is a really quick supper. The rice cooks merrily alongside the chick peas so that everything is ready at the same time.

Serves 4
Preparation time: 20 minutes
Cooking time: 20 minutes

350g (12¼oz) basmati rice

large pinch of saffron threads

4 medium-sized ripe tomatoes

4 tablespoons olive oil

¼ teaspoon paprika

¼ teaspoon cayenne pepper

¼ teaspoon ground ginger

¼ teaspoon cumin seeds, roughly crushed

1 cinnamon stick, broken in half

1 Spanish onion, grated

two 415g (14½oz) cans chick peas, drained

½ handful of fresh coriander leaves, coarsely chopped

½ handful of fresh mint, coarsely chopped

Maldon salt and freshly ground black pepper

- Bring a large saucepan of water to the boil and add the rice and saffron. Bring back to the boil, reduce the heat and simmer for 15–20 minutes until the rice is tender. Drain.

- Put the tomatoes in a bowl and cover with boiling water. Leave them for exactly 20 seconds then plunge them straight into cold water. Drain and skin the tomatoes then roughly chop their flesh.

- Heat the oil in a wok or frying pan. Add the paprika, cayenne pepper, ginger, cumin seeds and cinnamon stick and fry gently for 3–4 minutes to 'cook off' the spice flavour. Add the onion and sauté over a moderate heat for 5 minutes until soft and golden. Add the tomatoes, chick peas, fresh coriander and mint and 150ml (5fl oz) water. Simmer gently, covered, for 15 minutes. Season with salt and pepper.

- Divide the saffron rice between 4 warm serving plates. Pile the vegetables on top and serve immediately.

EACH SERVING CONTAINS
Kcals 670 • Protein 22g • Fat 17g (of which saturated 2g) • Carbohydrate 108g
Fibre 9g • Kcals from fat 23%

New Potatoes and Petits Pois with Pungent Green Sauce

Every time I go to Spain I eat a big selection of tapas, which always includes a sauce reminiscent of the one in this recipe. It is also fabulous tossed over fresh vegetables or as a dip for crunchy vegetables. Serve the potatoes with crusty bread and a salad.

Serves 4
Preparation time: 15 minutes
Cooking time: 20 minutes

4 garlic cloves

handful of fresh coriander leaves

1 green pepper, seeded and
   coarsely chopped

120ml (4fl oz) olive oil

2 tablespoons red wine vinegar

750g (1lb 10oz) new potatoes,
   unpeeled

200g (7oz) petits pois

Maldon salt and freshly ground
   black pepper

◆ Put the garlic and coriander in a food processor and process to a paste. Add the green pepper, oil and vinegar to the paste and process until smooth. Transfer to a bowl and season with salt and pepper. Cover and set aside.

◆ Put the potatoes in a large saucepan of boiling water and simmer for about 15 minutes until they are almost cooked but still just firm in the centre when pierced with a sharp knife. Add the petits pois and continue to simmer for about 5 minutes until the potatoes are tender. Drain.

◆ Transfer the potatoes and peas to a warm serving bowl, add the green sauce and coat well. Serve warm.

EACH SERVING CONTAINS
Kcals 390 • Protein 8g • Fat 23g (of which saturated 3g) • Carbohydrate 41g
Fibre 5g • Kcals from fat 53% • Good source of vitamins C and A

Vegan Lasagne

This is probably the closest I am going to get to a traditional recipe in this book. However, there is a reason why dishes like lasagne are always popular. They do work and they are a joy to eat. My vegan version is made of layers of creamy sauce, freshly cooked soft pasta, fresh green spinach, mushroom and nutmeg, and a vividly red tomato and garlic layer. Serve with chunks of fresh focaccia and little bowls of extra virgin olive oil to dip the bread in. The number of lasagne sheets you use will depend on the size of your ovenproof dish. Make sure the sheets are in even layers and that they don't overlap – if they do they will not cook properly and will taste tough and 'doughy'.

Serves 4
Preparation time: 15 minutes
Cooking time: about 50 minutes

3 tablespoons olive oil

30g (1oz) plain flour

600ml (1 pint) vegetable stock (see page 55)

handful of fresh flat-leaf parsley, roughly chopped

150g (5½oz) vegan cheese, grated

1 large onion, sliced

150g (5½oz) field mushrooms, thinly sliced

400g (14oz) fresh spinach, roughly chopped

pinch of grated fresh nutmeg

2 garlic cloves, crushed

2 tablespoons tomato purée

two 400g (14oz) cans chopped tomatoes

10–12 lasagne sheets

Maldon salt and freshly ground black pepper

◆ Preheat the oven to 200°C/400°F/Gas 6. Put 1 tablespoon olive oil and the flour and stock into a saucepan and whisk continuously over a gentle heat for about 5 minutes until thick and smooth. Season with salt and pepper and stir in the parsley and 75g (2½oz) cheese. Set aside.

◆ Heat 1 tablespoon olive oil in a wok or large frying pan. Add the onion and mushrooms and sauté over moderate heat for 5 minutes or until the onion is soft and golden. Add the spinach and cook for a minute until wilted. Season with salt, pepper and the nutmeg. Set aside.

◆ Heat the remaining oil in a large frying pan. Add the garlic and fry gently for 3 minutes. Add the tomato purée and tomatoes and simmer gently for 10 minutes until the mixture has reduced to a thick, vivid sauce.

▶

◆ Lightly oil an ovenproof dish and spread half the tomato sauce over the bottom. Cover with a layer of lasagne. Spread one-third of the white sauce on top of the lasagne, then spread half the spinach and mushroom sauce over the white sauce. Cover with a layer of lasagne. Repeat the process – you will end with a layer of lasagne topped with white sauce. Scatter the remaining grated cheese over the top and bake for 25–30 minutes until the topping is golden and bubbling. Serve immediately.

EACH SERVING CONTAINS
Kcals 550 • Protein 26g • Fat 29g (of which saturated 13g) • Carbohydrate 47g • Fibre 6g
Kcals from fat 49% • Excellent source of vitamins E, C and A • Good source of niacin, folic acid

Homemade Pizzas

There are many different ways of making pizza dough. This method is based on a recipe I learnt from an Italian who convinced me that it is the best. There is something very therapeutic about kneading pizza dough, but if you are not convinced put the toppings on ready-made pizza bases or focaccia breads. Italians do not believe in putting lots of different ingredients on one base – they just use a few good-quality ones. I've suggested two pizza toppings but you could invent your own: caramelize onions and make an onion pizza, or use a mixture of artichoke hearts, fresh tomatoes and olives. The only restriction is your imagination.

If you want to make sure that your pizzas have crispy bases, buy a pizza stone or tile, available from good kitchenware shops. '00' or '0' flour are best for making the dough and can be found in delicatessens or large supermarkets. However, if you can't find either of them, use strong white flour. You can use two 6g sachets of easy-blend yeast instead of fresh yeast: add it to the flour with the sugar and salt and mix the water and oil in afterwards.

Serves 4
Preparation time: 25 minutes, plus 1¼ hours for rising
Cooking time: 8–10 minutes

25g (¾oz) fresh yeast, crumbled
½ teaspoon sugar
1 teaspoon salt
500g (lb 2oz) flour (see above)
3 tablespoons extra virgin olive oil

For tomato and wild rocket topping
150g (5½oz) Cirio Rustica crushed tomatoes
Maldon salt
2 tablespoons extra virgin olive oil

large handful of fresh wild rocket leaves, roughly torn, *or* fresh basil leaves, roughly torn

For fresh garlic and rosemary topping
4 garlic cloves, sliced
4 sprigs of fresh rosemary
Maldon salt
3–4 tablespoons extra virgin olive oil

◆ Put 200ml (7fl oz) tepid water in a bowl. Stir in the yeast and sugar and leave for a couple of minutes until the yeast has dissolved. Mix the salt with the flour in a large bowl and make a well in the middle. Pour the yeast mixture into the well and use a wooden spoon to gradually bring the flour into the liquid from around the edges. When most of the flour is mixed in, slowly drizzle the oil into the middle of the flour mixture. Continue mixing

▶

in the flour until it forms a dough that comes away from the sides of the bowl – you may find it easier to use your hands at this stage. Remove the dough from the bowl, put it on a clean surface and knead it with your fingers and the palms of your hands for about 10–15 minutes until it is smooth, soft and silky.

◆ Put the dough into a clean bowl, cover with cling film and leave to rise in a warm place for 1 hour or until it has doubled in size. Knock the dough back and divide it into 2 balls. Cover the balls and leave them to rise for 10 minutes.

◆ Preheat the oven to 220°C/425° F/Gas 7. Shape each ball into a large circle about 23cm (9in) in diameter. Bring up the edges of each circle and pinch them to form a rim. Lightly oil 2 baking trays and transfer the circles to them. Prick the centres of the circles all over with a fork.

◆ To make the tomato and wild rocket pizza: Spoon the crushed tomatoes on to a pizza base, sprinkle with salt and drizzle the olive oil over the top. Bake for 10 minutes. Put the pizza under a hot grill for a few minutes if you want it to be more golden, then scatter the fresh rocket over the top and serve immediately.

◆ To make the fresh garlic and rosemary pizza: Scatter the garlic, rosemary and sea salt over a pizza base and drizzle the olive oil over the top. Bake for 8–10 minutes. Put the pizza under a hot grill if you want it to be more golden, then serve immediately.

EACH SERVING CONTAINS
Pizza with tomato and rocket: Kcals 560 • Protein 15g • Fat 15g (of which saturated 2g)
Carbohydrate 96g • Fibre 4g • Kcals from fat 25% • Good source of vitamin B₁
Pizza with fresh garlic and rosemary: Kcals 580 • Protein 15g • Fat 18g (of which saturated 2g)
Carbohydrate 96g • Fibre 4g • Kcals from fat 28% • Good source of vitamin D

desserts

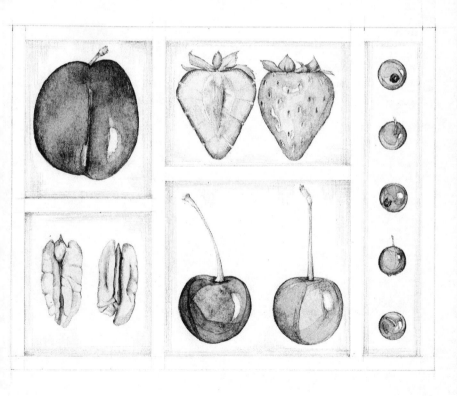

Warm Hazelnut Scones with Fruit Salsa

There is nothing quite like fresh hot scones straight from the oven – and you do not need cream or butter to make them tasty. A thick fruity salsa is simply delicious, and the contrast of warm and cold is sublime.

Serves 4
Preparation time: 15 minutes
Cooking time: 15 minutes

100g (3½oz) hazelnuts

225g (8oz) plain flour

40g (1½oz) vegan margarine

1½ tablespoons soft brown sugar

pinch of salt

155ml (5fl oz) soya milk

For the fruit salsa

225g (8oz) raspberries

grated zest and juice of 1 lime

♦ Preheat the oven to 225°C/425°F/Gas 7 and grease a baking sheet. Coarsely chop the hazelnuts and dry-fry them in a heavy-based frying pan over a moderate heat, turning or stirring frequently, for a couple of minutes or until golden.

♦ Sift the flour into a bowl and rub in the margarine using your fingertips. Stir in the sugar and salt, then use a knife to gradually mix in the milk. Then use your hands to lightly knead the mixture into a soft dough, adding a drop more milk if the mixture feels too dry.

♦ Turn the dough out on to a floured surface and roll it out to about 2cm (¾in) thick. Use a 5cm (2in) round cutter to cut out about 15 scones and place them on the baking sheet.

♦ Bake the scones for 12–15 minutes until well risen and golden brown. Mash the raspberries with the lime juice while the scones are baking.

♦ Break open the hot, freshly baked scones and spoon the salsa inside. Sprinkle a little zest over the fruit and sandwich the scones back together. Devour!

EACH SERVING CONTAINS
Kcals 470 • Protein 10g • Fat 26g (of which saturated 1.5g) • Carbohydrate 50g
Fibre 5g • Kcals from fat 51% • Excellent source of vitamins C and E

Coconut Rice Pudding with Mango and Papaya

There's a taste of the tropics in every mouthful of this dessert. It looks stunning and tastes as indulgent as any rice pudding, but without the fat! Save the papaya seeds and use them in a salad dressing – they are peppery and very good for the digestion.

Serves 4
Preparation time: 15 minutes
Cooking time: 15–20 minutes

150g (5½oz) pudding rice

250 ml (8½fl oz) soya milk

250 ml (8½fl oz) unsweetened
   coconut milk

½ teaspoon vanilla extract

25g (1oz) golden caster sugar

1 large ripe mango

1 large ripe papaya

handful of fresh basil leaves, to
   decorate

◆ Put the rice, soya milk, coconut milk and vanilla extract into a saucepan with 100ml (3½fl oz) water. Stir, then bring to the boil. Reduce the heat and simmer for 15–20 minutes until the rice is tender but still has a bite to it, stirring frequently to prevent the mixture sticking to the bottom. If necessary, add a few tablespoons of water to loosen the mixture. Add the sugar and mix well. Simmer for another minute.

◆ Peel the mango and use a sharp knife to slice the flesh away from the stone. Cut the flesh lengthways into thin slices. Slice the papaya in half and scoop out the seeds with a teaspoon and peel. Cut the flesh into thin slices.

◆ Divide the mango and papaya slices between 4 large plates and arrange the rice pudding next to them. Scatter fresh basil over the top and serve.

EACH SERVING CONTAINS
Kcals 295 • Protein 5g • Fat 9g (of which saturated 6g) • Carbohydrate 50g
Fibre 2g • Kcals from fat 27% • Excellent source of vitamin C

Moroccan Spiced Rice Pudding

Ingredients like almonds and dried fruits play a major role in Moroccan desserts. I love the combination of almonds, apricots and raisins, especially with the addition of a splash of orange-flower water (available from supermarkets).

Serves 4
Preparation time: 15 minutes
Cooking time: about 25 minutes

1.2 litres (2 pints) soya milk
50–75g (1¾–2½oz) pudding rice
2 tablespoons ground rice
170g (6oz) golden caster sugar
125g (4½oz) ground almonds
½ handful of dried apricots, soaked
    in orange-flower water to cover

½ handful of raisins, soaked in
    orange-flower water to cover
¼ teaspoon almond extract
½ teaspoon vanilla extract
2 tablespoons orange-flower water
pinch of ground cinnamon, for
    dusting

Put 900ml (1½ pints) soya milk in a saucepan and bring gently to the boil. Add the rice, reduce the heat and simmer for 15–20 minutes until the rice is tender but still has a bite to it, stirring frequently to prevent the mixture sticking to the bottom. If necessary, add a few tablespoons of water to loosen the mixture.

In a small bowl, mix the ground rice with about 2 tablespoons water – enough to make a smooth paste. Add the remaining milk to the paste and stir well. Pour the ground rice mixture into the saucepan with rice and bring to the boil over a low heat, stirring constantly. Add the sugar, ground almonds, apricots and raisins and simmer gently, stirring constantly, until the mixture thickens. Remove the saucepan from the heat and stir in the almond and vanilla extracts and the orange-flower water. Leave to cool for a few minutes.

Divide the rice pudding between 4 chunky tumblers and chill in the fridge for several hours. Dust with ground cinnamon and serve.

EACH SERVING CONTAINS
Kcals 560 • Protein 17g • Fat 23g (of which saturated 2g) • Carbohydrate 73g • Fibre 3g
Kcals from fat 37% • Excellent source of vitamin E • Good source of riboflavin, vitamin B_2

Baked Pears and Ginger

Pears are often poached but rarely baked. These ones taste delicious served with soya ice-cream or a scoop of Coconut Ice (see page 164). For extra colour, scatter a few fresh mint leaves over the top just before serving.

Serves 6
Preparation time: 10 minutes
Cooking time: 20–30 minutes

6 firm pears, such as Comice
juice of 1 lemon
1 rounded tablespoon golden
    caster sugar
1 teaspoon vanilla extract

4 pieces stem ginger preserved in
    syrup, drained and thinly sliced
2 tablespoons ginger syrup from
    the preserved stem ginger

◆ Preheat the oven to 200°C/400°F/Gas 6. Peel, halve and core the pears. Put them in a bowl, sprinkle the lemon juice over them and toss until they are well coated. Arrange the pears, cut side up, in an ovenproof dish.

◆ Put the sugar, vanilla extract, stem ginger and ginger syrup in the bowl that contained the pears. Mix with any left-over lemon juice and pour the mixture over the pears. Bake for 20–30 minutes, basting occasionally, until the pears are tender and golden at the edges. Serve warm or hot.

EACH SERVING CONTAINS
Kcals 90 • Protein 0.5g • Carbohydrate 22g • Fibre 4g

Hot Poached Pears with Toffee Crisps

I only add sugar to fruit desserts if absolutely necessary. Fruits have their own natural sugars and are very often sweet enough. However, they may need a little help if they are underripe, so taste before deciding whether additional sugar is needed. Pears are a great source of vitamin C. I eat a lot of fresh grapes and use grape juice in cooking. Grapes have been revered for many years as the queen of fruits because of their ability to cleanse and purify the body.

Serves 4
Preparation time: 25 minutes
Cooking time: 35 minutes

150ml (5fl oz) grape juice

2 tablespoons golden caster sugar

4 ripe pears

handful of fresh mint leaves,
   roughly torn, to decorate

For the toffee crisps

4 wheat tortillas, cut into 2.5cm
   (1in) strips

golden icing sugar, for dusting

♦ Put the grape juice and sugar in a saucepan (preferably stainless steel or enamelled cast iron) large enough to hold 4 pears. Heat gently to dissolve the sugar, then bring to a simmer.

♦ Meanwhile, peel the pears. Use a vegetable peeler and peel them from top to bottom, in strips, so that the fruit is smooth. Slice off the bottoms of the pears so that they sit easily. Sit the pears in the grape juice and simmer gently, frequently spooning the hot juice over the fruit, for about 30 minutes until tender. Remove the pears, bring the syrup to the boil and reduce by one-third.

♦ Meanwhile, make the toffee crisps: Preheat the grill to high. Place the tortilla strips on a baking tray and grill for 1 minute, until beginning to brown. Dust heavily with the golden icing sugar and return to the grill for another few minutes, or until the sugar has caramelized.

♦ Divide the pears between 4 plates and drizzle the syrup over them. Scatter fresh mint leaves over the the pears and serve with the toffee crisps.

EACH SERVING CONTAINS
Kcals 305 • Protein 4g • Fat negligible • Carbohydrate 75g • Fibre 4.5g • Kcals from fat 2.4%

Poached Fruits in Lavender-infused Syrup with Toffee Crisps

Lavender has only recently gained popularity in Britain as a culinary herb. I love its slightly aromatic flavour, especially in a light vanilla sugar syrup. The great thing about this recipe is that it can be made in advance and left to cool until needed – just pop the tortilla strips under the grill when you are nearly ready to eat. Like all food, the presentation is critical, so for a really stunning effect serve the fruits in wine glasses with a couple of toffee crisps at right angles to one another resting on the top of each glass.

Serves 4
Preparation time: 15 minutes
Cooking time: 25 minutes

125g (4½oz) golden caster sugar

flowers from 3 sprigs of lavender

1 vanilla pod, split

6 apricots

5 peaches

150ml (5fl oz) organic white wine

Toffee Crisps (see page 157)

♦ Put the sugar and 300ml (10fl oz) water into a saucepan (preferably stainless steel or enamelled cast iron) and heat gently to dissolve the sugar. Bring to the boil, add the lavender flowers and vanilla pod, and simmer for 10 minutes.

♦ Peel, stone and halve the apricots and peaches then cut them into quarters and slide the pieces into the syrup. Simmer gently until the fruit is tender. This will take about 5–10 minutes, depending on the ripeness of the fruit.

♦ Use a draining spoon to remove the fruit from the syrup, then divide the quarters between 4 glasses or dishes. Pour the wine into the syrup and stir, then strain the liquid on to the fruit and chill in the fridge. Serve the chilled lavender-infused fruits with hot toffee crisps.

EACH SERVING CONTAINS
Kcals 200 • Protein 2g • Carbohydrate 46g • Fibre 3g • Excellent source of vitamin C

Fruits with Cardamom and Vanilla

This is an excellent example of how fresh, tasty and exciting vegan desserts can be. It is important to remember that the longer you leave the spices in the syrup, the spicier it becomes. This may sound obvious, but if you leave them for half a day, the syrup will probably be a little too strong for your guests. It can be served with or without the spices. Experiment with other fruits in season.

Serves 4
Preparation time: 15 minutes
Cooking time: 15 minutes

75g (2½oz) golden caster sugar	120ml (4fl oz) orange juice
4 green cardamom pods	3 bananas
3 star anise	4 ripe peaches
couple of drops of vanilla extract	225g (8oz) blueberries
4 black peppercorns	

◆ Put the sugar in a saucepan (preferably stainless steel or enamelled cast iron) with 120ml (4fl oz) water and heat gently until the the sugar has dissolved. Add the cardamom, star anise, vanilla extract, peppercorns and orange juice. Bring to the boil, and simmer gently, covered, for 10 minutes. Remove from the heat and leave to cool.

◆ Peel the bananas, cut them diagonally into thick slices and divide them between 4 large soup plates. Peel, stone and thinly slice the peaches. Scatter the peach slices and blueberries over the bananas and drizzle the syrup over them. Serve.

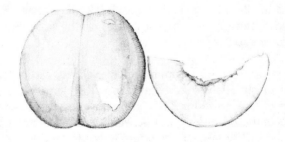

EACH SERVING CONTAINS
Kcals 200 • Protein 2g • Fat less than 1g (of which none is saturated) • Carbohydrate 50g
Fibre 4g • Kcals from fat 2% • Excellent source of vitamin C

Orange and Passionfruit Sorbet

I spent three years as a development chef for a company who produce ice-creams and sorbets and as a result I tend to be fussy when it comes to fruit sorbets or sherberts. To my mind there are at least two important criteria by which to judge them. First, a sorbet should taste of its ingredients – this may sound obvious, but it is fundamental and so often not the case. In this recipe, the strong passionfruit and orange flavour comes from using fresh fruits (which means a lot of oranges), rather than lots of water and very little fruit, to make the juice. Second, the texture must be smooth and creamy, not icy and crunchy. The best way to achieve this is to make the sorbet in an ice-cream machine which will freeze the mixture rapidly. If you don't have a machine, freeze the sorbet in a domestic freezer but remember to beat the mixture vigorously at intervals with a fork or electric whisk while it freezes in order to break down the ice crystals.

Serves 4
Preparation time: 20 minutes, plus freezing time
Cooking time: 5 minutes

---

2 kg (4½lb) oranges
250g (9oz) golden caster sugar
10 passion fruit

handful of fresh mint leaves,
roughly torn, to decorate

◆ Slice the oranges in half widthways and scoop out the flesh with a tablespoon. Put the flesh in a sieve and strain the juice into a large bowl, pressing the flesh firmly against the sieve. Put the juice in a saucepan (preferably stainless steel or enamelled cast iron), stir in the sugar and heat gently for about 5 minutes until the sugar has dissolved. Leave to cool.

◆ Slice 9 passionfruit in half widthways and scoop out the flesh with a teaspoon. Put the flesh in a jug and set aside 12 of the shells. Strain the juice into a bowl, pressing the pulp firmly against the sieve. Stir the passionfruit juice into the orange syrup.

◆ Transfer the syrup to an ice-cream machine and freeze according to the manufacturer's instructions. Alternatively, pour the syrup into a freezeproof container, cover and freeze for 2 hours. Remove the container from the freezer and beat the mixture vigorously with a fork or electric whisk to break down the ice crystals. Cover, return to the freezer, leave for a further

2 more hours and repeat the process. Cover, return the sorbet to the freezer and leave for 2–3 hours until it hardens.

◆ Use a teaspoon to scoop the sorbet into the reserved passionfruit shells; put 3 shells on each of 4 plates. Slice the remaining passion fruit in half and drizzle a little of its juice over the sorbets. Top each with fresh mint leaves and serve. Keep the remaining sorbet covered in the freezer.

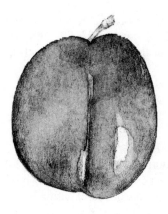

EACH SERVING CONTAINS
Kcals 44 • Protein 6g • Carbohydrate 110g • Excellent source of vitamin C
Good source of folic acid

Papaya and Coconut Sherbert

I describe this dessert as a sherbert because the creamed coconut and coconut shavings create a totally different eating experience. Serve it with fresh coconut, grated ginger and rum for a complete tropical sensation.

Serves 4
Preparation time: 20 minutes, plus freezing
Cooking time: 10 minutes

225g (8oz) golden caster sugar

4 ripe papaya, peeled, seeded and
    cut into chunks

85g (3oz) creamed coconut

5 tablespoons rum, plus extra for
    drizzling

grated zest of ½ lime

To decorate

handful of fresh coconut shavings

freshly grated fresh root ginger
    (optional)

◆ Put the sugar in a saucepan (preferably stainless steel or enamelled cast iron) with 225ml (7½fl oz) water and heat gently for 10 minutes until the sugar has dissolved. Pour the syrup into a large bowl and leave to cool.

◆ Put the papaya in a food processor and process to a smooth purée. Stir the purée, creamed coconut, rum and lime zest into the syrup and mix until smooth.

◆ Transfer the mixture to an ice-cream machine and freeze according to the manufacturer's instructions. Alternatively, pour it into a freezeproof container, cover and freeze for 2 hours. Remove the container from the freezer and beat the mixture vigorously with a fork or electric whisk to break down the ice crystals. Cover, return to the freezer, leave for a further hour and repeat the process. Cover, return the sherbert to the freezer and leave for at least 2 hours until it hardens.

◆ Dry-fry the coconut shavings in a heavy-based frying pan over a moderate heat, turning or stirring frequently, for a couple of minutes until just turning golden.

◆ Divide the sherbert between 4 tall glasses. Drizzle a little rum over each serving and scatter the coconut shavings and freshly grated ginger, if using, over the top. Serve.

EACH SERVING CONTAINS
Kcals 405 • Protein 1.5g • Fat 7g (of which saturated 6g) • Carbohydrate 77g • Fibre 5g
Kcals from fat 16% • Excellent source of vitamin C • Good source of vitamin A

Lemon Sherbert Cups with Crushed Blueberries

The combination of lemon sherbert and crushed blueberries makes a refreshing dessert. Alternatively, serve the sherbert on its own to cleanse the palate between courses. There is a higher than usual proportion of water in the sherbert because the flavour of the lemons would otherwise be too intense.

Serves 4
Preparation time: 20 minutes, plus freezing time
Cooking time: 5 minutes

---

3 large lemons, washed, plus 1 tablespoon lemon juice
185g (6½oz) golden caster sugar, plus 1 teaspoon

250g (8½oz) blueberries

◆ Peel the zest from 1 lemon and squeeze out its juice. Carefully cut the remaining lemons in half widthways and squeeze out their juice. Reserve the halves. In a large saucepan (preferably stainless steel or enamelled cast iron) mix the lemon zest, juice of all 3 lemons and sugar with 275ml (9fl oz) water. Heat gently for 5 minutes until the sugar has dissolved.

◆ Transfer the mixture to an ice-cream machine and freeze according to the manufacturer's instructions. Alternatively, pour it into a freezeproof container, cover and freeze for 2 hours. Remove the container from the freezer and beat the mixture vigorously with a fork or electric whisk to break down the ice crystals. Cover, return to the freezer, leave for a further hour and repeat the process. Cover, return the sherbert to the freezer and leave for at least 2 hours until it hardens.

◆ Crush the blueberries and mix them with 1 tablespoon lemon juice and 1 teaspoon sugar or to taste. Divide the sherbert between the lemon halves, drizzle the crushed blueberries over the centre of each one and serve.

EACH SERVING CONTAINS
Kcals 200 • Protein 0.5g • Carbohydrate 52g • Fibre 2g • Excellent source of vitamin C

Coconut Ice Dessert with Chocolate Sauce

Although this is not technically an ice-cream it behaves and tastes just like one. I am proud of this recipe – it is always pleasing to achieve a fabulous flavour and texture without using cream and other dairy ingredients. I've twinned it with a chocolate sauce here – if you wish, you could ripple the sauce through the frozen ice rather than serving it separately – but you could also serve the ice with chopped fresh mango and papaya. If you can find a fresh coconut, toast shavings of the flesh and scatter them over it. And, of course, it's good on its own.

Serves 4
Preparation time: 20 minutes, plus freezing time
Cooking time: 5 minutes

600ml (1 pint) soya milk

1 vanilla pod, split

125g (4½oz) shredded coconut

2 tablespoons custard powder

125g (4½oz) golden caster sugar

400ml (14fl oz) can unsweetened coconut milk

For the chocolate ripple

2 heaped tablespoons cocoa powder

2 heaped tablespoons soft brown sugar

3 tablespoons golden syrup

◆ Put the soya milk and vanilla pod in a saucepan and bring to the boil. Turn the heat off, cover and leave the milk to infuse.

◆ Dry-fry the shredded coconut in a heay-based frying pan over a moderate heat, turning or stirring frequently, for a few minutes until golden.

◆ Meanwhile, put the custard powder and sugar in a small bowl. Add about 2 tablespoons of the hot milk and mix to a paste. Stir the paste into the infused milk in the saucepan, and bring back to the boil, stirring constantly, for at least 5 minutes or until the milk thickens. Add the coconut milk and shredded coconut and stir well. Leave to cool.

◆ Transfer the mixture to an ice-cream machine and freeze according to the manufacturer's instructions. Alternatively, pour it into a freezeproof container, cover and freeze for 2 hours. Remove the container from the freezer and beat the mixture vigorously with a fork or electric whisk to break down the ice crystals. Cover, return to the freezer, leave for a further 2 hours.

◆ Make the chocolate ripple: Put the cocoa powder, sugar and golden syrup in a saucepan with 120ml (4fl oz) water and heat gently until the cocoa and sugar have dissolved. Bring to the boil then reduce the heat and simmer gently for 2–3 minutes until thick.

◆ Divide the coconut ice between 4 bowls or glasses and serve the hot chocolate sauce as an accompaniment.

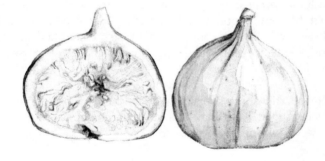

EACH SERVING CONTAINS
Kcals 495 • Protein 6g • Fat 26g (of which saturated 20g) • Carbohydrate 59g
Fibre 3g • Kcals from fat 47%

Frozen Yogurt Crunch with Raspberry Sauce

This may seem childish, but adults love this dessert as much as children. Make it and keep it in the freezer until you fancy a sweet fix. I developed this recipe one day when I put some biscuits and jam into the freezer – I am a firm believer that most creations happen when you least expect them to. I have used ginger snaps here, but any sweet biscuits will do. Just check the label to make sure they are vegan. Similarly, the frozen yogurt can be replaced by soya ice-cream.

Serves 4
Preparation time: 20 minutes

250g (9oz) crunchy cereal

150g (5½oz) ginger snaps

3 tablespoons low-sugar fruit jam

300g (10½oz) frozen vanilla soya
    yogurt

250g (9oz) raspberries

dash of lime juice

1 teaspoon golden icing sugar

◆ Finely crush the cereal and ginger snaps with a rolling pin, then mix the crumbs with the jam. Spoon the mixture into 24 small paper cases and press it down firmly. Fill the cases with the frozen yogurt and cover them with foil or cling film. Arrange the cases on a baking tray and freeze for 20 minutes.

◆ Push the raspberries through a sieve with a wooden spoon. Stir in the lime juice and icing sugar. Serve the cases of yogurt crunch with a jug of raspberry sauce for drizzling over them.

EACH SERVING CONTAINS
Kcals 565 • Protein 9g • Fat 17g (of which saturated 5.5g) • Carbohydrate 96g
Fibre 12g • Kcals from fat 28% • Good source of vitamin C

Fresh Fruits in Wine with Basil

For a really light and dazzling dessert, serve the fruits in wine glasses with just enough wine to cover them. Fresh basil has a wonderful sweet and subtle flavour – I often scatter it over a plate of fresh strawberries or other soft fruits for a very simple, elegant dessert. The amount of wine you use will depend on the size of your glasses – you may not need the whole bottle.

Serves 4
Preparation time: 20 minutes

1 large ripe mango

1 large ripe papaya

450g (1lb) strawberries, hulled and
   sliced

2 bananas, peeled and sliced

4 apricots, stoned and sliced

1 bottle organic white wine

handful of fresh basil leaves, to
   decorate

◆ Peel the mango and use a sharp knife to slice the flesh away from the stone. Cut the flesh into thin slices about 5cm (2in) long and put it in a bowl. Slice the papaya in half lengthways, scoop out the seeds with a teaspoon, and peel. Cut the flesh into thin slices about 5cm (2in) long and add them to the mango. Add the strawberries, bananas and apricots and mix well.

◆ Divide the fruits between 4 wine glasses. Pour enough wine over them to cover, scatter fresh basil on top and serve.

EACH SERVING CONTAINS
Kcals 250 • Protein 2.5g • Carbohydrate 30g • Fibre 4g • Excellent source of vitamin C

Strawberries with Black Pepper

The simplicity of this dessert appeals to me. It may seem a strange combination, but the pepper really enhances the fruity strawberry flavour. Use fresh English strawberries when they are in season or, better still, wild strawberries bursting with ten times more flavour than large ones grown commercially.

Serves 4
Preparation time: 20 minutes

450g (1lb) strawberries, hulled and thinly sliced

3 blood oranges
freshly ground black pepper

◆ Arrange the strawberries in a single layer on 4 plates. Peel 2 oranges with a sharp knife, making sure you remove all the white pith, then cut the flesh into thin slices. Arrange the orange slices in between the strawberries so that you can see both fruits. Cut the remaining orange in half and squeeze the juice over the fruit. Grind a sprinkling of pepper over each serving.

EACH SERVING CONTAINS
Kcals 78 • Protein 2g • Carbohydrate 17g • Fibre 3g • Excellent source of vitamin C

Toffee Figs with a Glass of Brandy

To me, fresh figs are one of the most sensual fruits in the world. Choose ones that are soft to touch with a fruity (not sour) smell. Figs are sometimes criticized for their lack of sweetness, which may be why they are often turned into fig puddings or biscuits. Any sceptics should give these ones a go – encased in a sweet crisp caramel they are too good to ignore.

Serves 4
Preparation time: 20 minutes
Cooking time: 20 minutes

340g (12oz) golden caster sugar
¼ teaspoon lemon juice

450g (1lb) fresh figs, at room temperature

◆ Put the sugar and lemon juice in a small heavy-based saucepan with 120ml (4fl oz) water. Swirl the water around in the pan to make sure all the sugar is immersed. Heat gently until the sugar has dissolved, swirling the pan occasionally. Continue to heat gently until the sugar solution turns a golden-brown colour.

◆ When the syrup has caramelized to a light golden brown, remove the pan from the heat. Using 2 forks, dip the figs one at a time into the syrup. Shake off the excess caramel – the coating must be thin and even – and arrange the fruit immediately on serving plates (you will not be able to move them once the caramel sets). Work quickly: the caramel will thicken as the figs cool it down. If this happens, reheat it gently before continuing. Serve the figs with a glass of brandy.

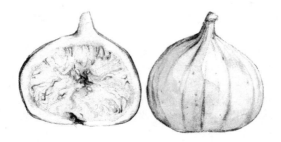

EACH SERVING CONTAINS
Kcals 380 • Protein 1g • Carbohydrate 100g • Fibre 1.5g

Caramelized Oranges with Cranberries

Dried fruits like cranberries are available all year round and well worth keeping in the storecupboard at all times. Throw a handful into scones, biscuits or sauces like this one. The dried berries have a very intense flavour and because the water has been removed the sugar is concentrated, making them deliciously sweet. Make sure you remove all the bitter white pith when you peel the oranges.

Serves 4

Preparation time: 30 minutes, plus 2–3 hours chilling time
Cooking time: 10–15 minutes

55g (2oz) dried cranberries
9 medium-sized juicy oranges
225g (8oz) golden caster sugar

2 tablespoons Grand Marnier *or* brandy

◆ Put the cranberries in a bowl. Squeeze the juice from 1 orange and pour it over the cranberries. Remove the zest from 4 oranges with a zester or vegetable peeler. Bring a small saucepan of water to the boil, add the zest and blanch for a couple of seconds. Drain. Add the zest to the soaking cranberries. Set aside.

◆ Use a sharp serrated knife to cut the skins and pith from the remaining oranges. Carefully follow the curve of the fruit, working in small downward sections. Hold the oranges over a bowl as you work, to catch any juices. Slice the oranges into rounds (discarding any pips) and put them in a bowl.

◆ Put the sugar in a saucepan with 300ml (10fl oz) water. Swirl the water around in the pan to make sure all the sugar is immersed. Heat gently until the sugar has dissolved, swirling the pan occasionally. Bring to the boil and continue to boil until the syrup is golden. Watch carefully – if the caramel is too dark it will taste bitter. Leave to cool slightly.

◆ Arrange the orange slices in a serving dish. Carefully stir any juices left in the bowl, and any juices left over from peeling the oranges, into the caramel. Stir in the Grand Marnier or brandy. Leave the caramel to cool for a further 10 minutes then pour it over the oranges. Add the cranberres and mix carefully. Refrigerate for 2–3 hours before serving.

EACH SERVING CONTAINS
Kcals 415 • Protein 4.5g • Fat less than 1g (of which none is saturated) • Carbohydrate 100g
Fibre 5g • Kcals from fat1% • Excellent source of vitamin C

Orange Custards with Cherry Jam

This custard is also great served with fruit crisps. For a vanilla version, leave out the orange zest and juice and add a fresh vanilla bean or vanilla extract to the milk. Soya milk contains no cholesterol and is the ideal substitute for dairy milk. Check the label on the custard powder packet to make sure it does not include animal-derived products.

Serves 4
Preparation time: 20 minutes
Cooking time: 20 minutes

---

2 tablespoons custard powder

1 tablespoon soft brown sugar

600ml (1 pint) soya milk

grated zest and juice of ½ orange

For the cherry jam

125g (4½oz) cherries, stoned

3 tablespoons golden caster sugar

few drops of lime juice

◆ Make the cherry jam: Put the cherries in a saucepan and warm gently for 5 minutes until the juices begin to run. Crush the cherries with a potato masher, then raise the heat and bring the juices to the boil. Stir in the sugar and lime juice and boil rapidly for about 10 minutes until the liquid thickens, stirring frequently. To test for a set, put a teaspoon of jam on a plate and put the plate in the freezer for 2 minutes. Remove the plate from the freezer and push the jam with your finger. If a crinkly skin forms on the jam it is the right consistency. Remove the saucepan from the heat and leave to cool.

◆ Combine the custard powder and sugar with about 2 tablespoons milk – just enough to form a smooth paste. Bring the remaining milk up to boiling point. Stir the paste into the hot milk and whisk over a gentle heat, without boiling, until the custard is thick and smooth. Mix in the orange zest and juice.

◆ Divide the custard between 4 little pots, put a dollop of cherry jam in the middle of each and serve warm or cold.

EACH SERVING CONTAINS
Kcals 150 • Protein 5g • Fat 3g (of which saturated 0.5g) • Carbohydrate 27g • Kcals from fat 18%

Plum and Cinnamon Crisp

This plum crumble has a little orange zest and cinnamon mixed into the crispy topping. If you prefer, it can be made in four individual ovenproof dishes instead of one large one.

Serves 4
Preparation time: 20 minutes
Cooking time: 40 minutes

700g (1½lb) fresh ripe plums, stoned and quartered

150g (5½oz) golden caster sugar

170g (6oz) plain flour

grated zest of ½ orange

1 teaspoon ground cinnamon

pinch of freshly grated nutmeg

pinch of salt

75g (2½oz) vegan margarine, chilled

◆ Preheat the oven to 190°C/375°F/Gas 5. Grease an ovenproof dish. Arrange the plums cut sides up in the dish. Combine 1 tablespoon sugar and 1 tablespoon flour and sift them over the plums.

◆ Put the remaining sugar and flour in a bowl and the add orange zest, cinnamon, nutmeg and salt. Cut the margarine into small pieces and, using your fingertips, rub it into the flour until the mixture resembles breadcrumbs. Sprinkle the topping over the plums.

◆ Transfer to the oven and bake for 40 minutes until the topping is crisp and golden brown and the plums are soft and juicy. Serve warm.

Apple and pear crisp
Replace the plums with 700g (1½lb) peeled, cored and sliced apples, and 225g (8oz) peeled, cored and sliced pears.

Nectarine and berry crisp
Replace the plums with 700g (1½lb) stoned, halved and thickly sliced nectarines, and 450g (1lb) raspberries. Add 50g (1¾oz) roughly chopped, toasted walnuts to the topping and omit the cinnamon.

EACH SERVING CONTAINS
Plum and cinnamon crisp: Kcals 500 • Protein 5g • Fat 16g (of which saturated 5g)
Carbohydrate 90g • Fibre 4.5g • Kcals from fat 29%
Apple and pear crisp: Kcals 735 • Protein 12g • Fat 37g (of which saturated 6g) • Carbohydrate 93g
Fibre 8g • Kcals from fat 46% • Excellent source of vitamin C
Nectarine and berry crisp: Kcals 670 • Protein 8g • Fat 28g (of which saturated 6g)
Carbohydrate 100g • Fibre 6g • Kcals from fat 39%

Pancakes

The Vegan Society gave me this recipe. Serve the pancakes in the traditional way with lemon juice and sugar, or with Fresh Fruit Compote (see page 178); Apricot Sauce (see page 184); or Apple and Brandy Sauce (see page 179). For a savoury dish, serve them with any of the following recipes: Puréed Chick Peas (see page 31); Warm Butter Bean Purée (see page 32); Rich Mushrooms (see page 37); Avocado with Beans and Coriander (see page 44); Avocado Butter (see page 94); Aubergine Butter (see page 136). Add a pinch of sugar to the mixture for sweet pancakes. For savoury pancakes you can season with salt and pepper or fresh herbs.

Serves 4
Preparation time: 10 minutes, plus chilling time
Cooking time: about 15 minutes

125g (4½oz) wholemeal flour

50g (1¾oz) soya flour

250ml (8½fl oz) soya milk

2 teaspoons vegetable oil

vegetable oil, for frying

lemon juice and golden caster
   sugar, to serve

◆ Sieve the wholemeal and soya flours into a large mixing bowl. Gradually add the soya milk, whisking vigorously with a fork to prevent lumps forming, to make a smooth batter. Whisk in the oil. Chill for 30 minutes.

◆ Preheat the oven to 150°C/300°F/Gas 2. Heat a little oil in a frying pan. As soon as it is hot pour 2 tablespoons of the batter into the centre of the pan. Swirl it around to form a thin pancake and cook for 1 minute until the underside is brown. Turn the pancake over and cook the other side. Transfer to a warm serving plate and continue until the batter is finished. Interleave the pancakes with sheets of greaseproof paper and keep them warm in the oven. Serve with lemon juice and sugar to taste.

EACH SERVING CONTAINS
Kcals 245 • Protein 10g • Fat 13g (of which saturated 1.5g) • Carbohydrate 23g
Fibre 4g • Kcals from fat 47%

Caramelized Peach and Almond Tart

This tart also works well if you smooth a few tablespoons of Orange Custard (see page 171) over the base of the pastry case before adding the fresh peaches. You could also replace the peaches with other fruits.

Serves 4–6
Preparation time: 20 minutes
Cooking time: 50 minutes

225g (8oz) ready-made shortcrust
    pastry, thawed if frozen
600g (1lb 5oz) ripe peaches
2 tablespoons golden icing sugar

30g (1oz) almonds
2 tablespoons apricot jam
1–2 tablespoons Kirsch

◆ Preheat the oven to 190°C/375°F/Gas 5. Roll the pastry out to a thickness of about 5mm (¼in). Line a 23cm (9in) flan tin with the pastry and prick the base all over with a fork. Chill for 30 minutes. Cover the pastry with greaseproof paper and baking beans and bake blind for 20–25 minutes until golden and crisp.

◆ Peel the peaches and cut them in half widthways. Remove the stones and slice the flesh thinly. Arrange the slices in the pre-baked pastry case so that they overlap slightly. Dust the slices with the sugar, return to the oven and bake for 30 minutes until the sugar is golden.

◆ Meanwhile, roughly chop the almonds and dry-fry them in a heavy-based frying pan over a moderate heat, turning or stirring frequently, for 5 minutes until golden. Scatter the almonds over the cooked tart.

◆ Put the jam and Kirsch in a small saucepan and warm gently for 5 minutes until the jam has melted. Brush the jam over the peaches and serve the tart warm.

EACH SERVING CONTAINS
4 servings: Kcals 395 • Protein 6g • Fat 20g (of which saturated 6g) • Carbohydrate 51g
Fibre 4g • Kcals from fat 45% • Good source of vitamin C
6 servings: Kcals 265 • Protein 4g • Fat 13g (of which saturated 4g) • Carbohydrate 34g
Fibre 2.5g • Kcals from fat 45% • Good source of vitamin C

Pecan and Butternut Squash Tart

It is always satisfying to develop a new pastry recipe that doesn't need butter to give it a rich, soft, crumbly texture. The combination of lots of nuts with maple syrup and tahini is delicious. I recommend using the recipe for the base for other tarts and pies. Or make little tarts and fill them with jam for a nutty sweet experience.

Serves 6
Preparation time: 25 minutes
Cooking time: 1 hour

3 small butternut squash	*For the pastry*
60ml (2fl oz) maple syrup	115g (4oz) pecans
juice of 1 lemon	140g (5oz) sunflower seeds
1 teaspoon ground cinnamon	85g (3oz) sesame seeds
¼ teaspoon ground cloves	2 tablespoons tahini
1 teaspoon vanilla extract	120ml (4fl oz) maple syrup
85g (3oz) pecans	60–120ml (2–4fl oz) sunflower oil
golden icing sugar, to dust	

◆ Preheat the oven to 180°C/350°F/Gas 4. Cut each butternut squash in half lengthways and scoop out all the seeds with a teaspoon. Put the squash, cut side down, on a baking tray and bake for 30–40 minutes or until the flesh is soft.

◆ Meanwhile, put all the pastry ingredients in a food processor and process to a thick smooth dough. Remove the dough from the processor and use your hands to flatten it to a 23cm (9in) circle. Line a 20cm (8in) pie dish with the dough, pressing it down well, prick all over with a fork and bake for 15–20 minutes until golden brown.

◆ Peel the butternut squash. Rinse out the bowl of the food processor. Put the flesh of the butternut squash and the maple syrup, lemon, cinnamon, cloves, vanilla extract and 120ml (4fl oz) water in the food processor and process until well mixed. Spoon the filling into the pastry-lined pie dish and decorate with the pecans. Bake for 15 minutes. Leave to cool slightly, dust with icing sugar and cut into slices. Serve.

EACH SERVING CONTAINS
Kcals 730 • Protein 14g • Fat 55g (of which saturated 5g) • Carbohydrate 47g • Fibre 8g
Kcals from fat 67% • Excellent source of vitamins B$_1$, niacin, C, A and E • Good source of folic acid

Treacle Tart

This recipe proves that a treacle tart doesn't have to be full of butter and other dairy products to taste rich and gooey. This one is delicious served hot with a scoop of soya ice-cream melting on top. You can replace half the golden syrup with treacle – and add a handful (50g/1¾oz) of toasted walnuts.

Serves 4
Preparation time:15 minutes, plus 30 minutes chilling time
Cooking time: 25 minutes

175g (6½oz) ready-made shortcrust
    pastry, thawed if frozen
225g (8oz) golden syrup
finely grated zest and juice of 1
    lemon

75g (2½oz) fresh white
    breadcrumbs

◆ Roll the pastry out on a lightly floured surface to a thickness of about 5mm (¼in). Line a 20cm (8in) flan tin with the pastry and prick the base all over with a fork. Chill for 30 minutes.

◆ Meanwhile preheat the oven to 190°C/375°F/Gas mark 5. Warm the syrup gently in a saucepan, then add the lemon zest and juice. Scatter the breadcrumbs over the pastry base and slowly pour in the syrup. Bake in the oven for 25 minutes until the filling is just set. Serve warm.

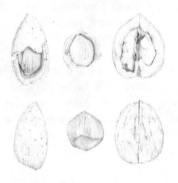

EACH SERVING CONTAINS
Kcals 430 • Protein 5g • Fat 12g (of which saturated 4g) • Carbohydrate 79g
Fibre 1g • Kcals from fat 26%

Baked Bananas with Orange and Hazelnuts

This is a hot version of a banana sundae. As with all nuts, dry-frying the hazelnuts really brings out their flavour.

Serves 4
Preparation time: 15 minutes
Cooking time: 20 minutes

4 firm bananas, unpeeled

1 tablespoon lemon juice

125g (4½oz) hazelnuts, roughly
   chopped

4 scoops soya ice-cream

juice of ½ orange

♦ Preheat the oven to 200°C/400°F/Gas 6. Put the bananas on a baking tray, brush them with the lemon juice and bake for 20 minutes or until they are dark and soft.

♦ Meanwhile, dry-fry the hazelnuts in a heavy-based frying pan over a moderate heat, turning or stirring frequently, for 5 minutes until golden. Roughly chop the nuts.

♦ Snip open the banana skins with scissors or a knife and put a scoop of ice-cream in the middle of each one. Drizzle the orange juice over the ice-cream and scatter the hazelnuts on top. Serve immediately.

EACH SERVING CONTAINS
Kcals 400 • Protein 7.5g • Fat 25g (of which saturated 4g)
Carbohydrate 39g • Fibre 3g • Kcals from fat 56%

Banana Flapjacks with Fresh Fruit Compote

The protein in brazil nuts is high in methionine, the amino acid that is often in shortest supply in a vegan diet. More important, the flapjacks look as tempting as they taste. Serve them on individual plates, as I suggest, or pile them up on a large dish and accompany with a bowl of the compote.

Makes 12 flapjacks
Preparation time: 20 minutes
Cooking time: 25–30 minutes

50g (1¾oz) brazil nuts, roughly chopped

115g (4oz) margarine

75g (2½oz) soft brown sugar

2 tablespoons golden syrup

375g (13oz) porridge oats

½ teaspoon baking powder

2 ripe bananas, mashed

For the compote

450g (1lb) fresh strawberries, hulled

115g (4oz) blueberries

115g (4oz) blackberries

115g (4oz) raspberries

4 teaspoons sugar

½ teaspoon Kirsch

◆ Preheat the oven to 180°C/350°F/Gas 4. Make the compote: Combine the strawberries, blueberries, blackberries and raspberries in a bowl. Sprinkle in the sugar and Kirsch and mix well. Chill until needed.

◆ Dry-fry the brazil nuts in a heavy-based frying pan over a moderate heat, turning or stirring frequently, for 5 minutes until golden.

◆ Lightly grease a 23 × 33cm (9 × 13in) Swiss roll tin. Put the margarine, sugar and syrup in a large saucepan and stir over a low heat for 5 minutes until melted. Mix in the brazil nuts, porridge oats and baking powder. Add the bananas and mix well. Spread the mixture out on the Swiss roll tin and bake for 20 minutes or until the edges are beginning to go golden. Cut into squares while still warm. Leave to cool slightly on the tin then transfer to a wire rack to finish cooling.

◆ Divide the flapjacks between 4 plates, add a spoonful of compote to each portion and serve.

EACH SERVING CONTAINS
Kcals 620 • Protein 10g • Fat 27g (of which saturated 6g) • Carbohydrate 88g • Fibre 7g
Kcals from fat 39% • Excellent source of vitamin C • Good source of vitamins E, B₁ (thiamine)

Walnut Layer with Apple and Brandy Sauce

Handle the walnut dough lightly so that it is crisp and light when cooked. The more you handle it, the harder and tougher it will become.

Serves 4
Preparation time: 20–25 minutes
Cooking time: 15–17 minutes

100g (3½oz) walnuts

115g (4oz) margarine

55g (2oz) soft brown sugar

115g (4oz) self-raising flour

4 tablespoons golden caster sugar

golden icing sugar, for dusting

For the apple and brandy sauce

1.1kg (2½lb) apples

juice of 1 lemon

2 tablespoons Calvados

1 tablespoon sugar

2 tablespoons apple jelly

◆ Preheat the oven to 180°C/350°F/Gas 4. Preheat the grill to high. Spread the walnuts on a baking tray and toast them under the grill for 5 minutes or until golden. Leave to cool, then chop finely.

◆ Lightly grease a baking sheet. Put the margarine and soft brown sugar in a bowl and beat well with a wooden spoon until light and fluffy. Add half the walnuts and the flour and, using your hands, work them together to form a dough that comes away from the sides of the bowl. Gently knead the dough until smooth. Transfer the dough to a floured surface and lightly roll it out to form a rectangle about 5mm (¼in) thick. Use an upturned plate to cut 2 circles about 15cm (6in) in diameter. Place the pastry circles on the baking sheet and bake for 10–12 minutes until pale golden. Use the point of a knife to lightly mark each circle into quarters. Sprinkle the caster sugar over the circles and leave to cool until crisp.

◆ Make the apple and brandy sauce: Peel the apples and cut into small chunks. Toss in lemon juice. Put the apples and brandy in a saucepan. Cover, bring to a simmer and simmer for 15 minutes. Add the sugar and apple jelly and simmer, stirring, for 5 minutes or until the apples form a thick purée.

◆ Slice each pastry circle into quarters along the marked lines. Put 1 quarter on a plate, spread 2 tablespoons apple and brandy sauce over it and cover with another quarter. Spoon a little sauce over the top. Sprinkle with a few of the remaining walnuts and dust with golden icing sugar. Repeat with the remaining pastry quarters and sauce and serve.

EACH SERVING CONTAINS
Kcals 785 • Protein 7g • Fat 41g (of which saturated 8g) • Carbohydrate 100g
Fibre 6g • Kcals from fat 47% • Good source of vitamins C and A

Sponge Cake with Strawberries and Lemon Balm

The Vegan Society swears by this recipe. The cake is both light and rich – and perfect when it is filled with fresh berries and a little sweet jam. I have used lemon balm leaves but fresh mint leaves are just as good. I never like to give quantities of sugar to add to fruits. Their sweetness level varies so much that it is best to sweeten them to taste.

Serves 6–8
Preparation time: 20 minutes
Cooking time: 25–30 minutes

125g (4½oz) margarine

75g (2½oz) golden caster sugar

250g (9oz) self-raising flour

3 teaspoons baking powder

pinch of Maldon salt

275ml (9fl oz) soya yogurt

¼ teaspoon vanilla extract

1–2 tablespoons soya milk

For the filling

450g (1lb) strawberries, sliced

sugar and orange liqueur, to taste

4 tablespoons strawberry jam

To decorate

golden icing sugar, for dusting

handful of lemon balm leaves

◆ Preheat the oven to 180°C/350°F/Gas 4. Put the margarine and sugar in a saucepan and heat gently until the sugar has dissolved. Leave to cool.

◆ Grease a 20cm (8in) cake tin and line the base with greaseproof paper. Sieve the flour and baking powder into a bowl and add the salt. Pour the margarine and sugar into the dry ingredients and add the yogurt and vanilla extract. Mix well with a wooden spoon until the mixture reaches a soft dropping consistency. Add a little soya milk if necessary. Spoon the cake mixture into the tin and bake for 20–25 minutes until risen and golden. The centre should feel springy if you touch it with your fingertips. Leave to cool.

◆ Cut the cake in half widthways. Put the strawberries into a bowl and add sugar and orange liqueur to taste. Spread a layer of jam over the tops of both halves of the cake. Cover one half with a layer of half the sliced strawberries and put the other half, jam side up, over it. Arrange the remaining berries on the jam and dust with icing sugar. Scatter a few fresh lemon balm leaves over the top and serve.

EACH SERVING CONTAINS
6 servings: Kcals 480 • Protein 6.5g • Fat 19g (of which saturated 8g) • Carbohydrate 73g
Fibre 2g • Kcals from fat 37% • Excellent source of vitamin C • Good source of vitamin A
8 servings: Kcals 360 • Protein 5g • Fat 14.5g (of which saturated 6g) • Carbohydrate 55g
Fibre 1.5g • Kcals from fat 37% • Excellent source of vitamin C • Good source of vitamin A

Chocolate Raspberry Hazelnut Cake

This is a chocolate cake for vegans that tastes as good as any I've ever tasted. I decided that I would not include a chocolate cake unless it was really chocolately, absolutely delicious and, more important, gooey in the middle as all good chocolate cakes are. This one is all these and more. It can be served hot with crushed raspberries as a dessert, or cold with a cup of tea in the middle of the afternoon. It is important to use frozen, not fresh, raspberries as they keep their shape much better.

Serves 10
Preparation time: 20 minutes
Cooking time: 45 minutes

55g (2oz) hazelnuts

250g (9oz) self-raising flour

85g (3oz) cocoa powder

3 teaspoons baking powder

250g (9oz) golden caster sugar

1½ teaspoons vanilla extract
  (optional)

120ml (4fl oz) corn oil

360ml (12fl oz) soya milk

125g (4½oz) frozen raspberries

golden icing sugar, for dusting

◆ Preheat the oven to 180°C/350°F/Gas 4. Preheat the grill to high. Spread the hazelnuts on a baking tray and toast them under the grill, turning frequently, for 5 minutes or until golden. Cool, then chop finely. Grease a 20cm (8in) cake tin and line the base with greaseproof paper.

◆ Sift the flour, cocoa powder and baking powder into a bowl. Mix in the sugar, then add the vanilla extract, if using, oil and soya milk. Beat the mixture with an electric whisk until it has the consistency of a thick batter. Stir in the raspberries and hazelnuts. Pour into the cake tin and bake for 40 minutes until the outside of the cake is cooked and the centre is still slightly squidgy. Cool on a wire rack. Alternatively, serve the cake warm as a dessert. Either way, dust the top with icing sugar before serving.

EACH SERVING CONTAINS
Kcals 335 • Protein 6g • Fat 15g (of which saturated 3g) • Carbohydrate 47g
Fibre 2.5g • Kcals from fat 40% • Good source of vitamin E

Winter Fruit Salad

Imagine hot fruits soaked in a rich sauce made of brandy, orange juice and ginger syrup and served in wine glasses. A cinnamon stick popped into each glass and a sprinkling of ground cinnamon provide the kind of finishing touch that transforms a traditional dish into something modern and fresh.

Serves 4
Preparation time: 20 minutes
Cooking time: 1 hour

55g (2oz) dried prunes, stoned

2 Cox's apples, peeled, cored and thinly sliced

55g (2oz) dried figs

55g (2oz) dried apricots

1 small pineapple, peeled, cored and diced

2 tablespoons Calvados *or* brandy of your choice

juice and zest of 1 orange

1 tablespoon ginger syrup from the preserved stem ginger (see below)

30g (1oz) golden caster sugar

To decorate

large handful of cashew nuts

large handful of hazelnuts

1 piece of stem ginger preserved in syrup, drained and cut into fine strips

4 cinnamon sticks

large pinch of ground cinnamon

♦ Preheat the oven to 180°C/350°F/Gas 4. Put the prunes, apples, figs, apricots, pineapple, Calvados or brandy, orange zest and juice, ginger syrup and sugar in an ovenproof dish. Mix well. Cover with a lid or aluminium foil and bake for 1 hour.

♦ Meanwhile, preheat the grill to high. Spread the cashew nuts and hazelnuts on a baking tray and toast them under the grill, turning frequently, for 5 minutes or until golden. Cool, then chop roughly.

♦ Divide the hot fruits between 4 wine glasses. Scatter the toasted cashew nuts and hazelnuts and the stem ginger strips over the top. Pop a cinnamon stick into each glass, sprinkle with ground cinnamon and serve.

EACH SERVING CONTAINS
Kcals 235 • Protein 3g • Fat 5g (of which saturated 0.5g) • Carbohydrate 43g
Fibre 5g • Kcals from fat 18% • Good source of vitamin C

Apricot and Raspberry Cobbler

A comforting and delicious pudding. You can substitute seasonal fruits for the apricots and raspberries – pears and blackberries work well, as do apples and blueberries. Serve with soya yogurt.

Serves 4
Preparation time: 20 minutes
Cooking time: 35–45 minutes

675g (1½lb) fresh apricots, stoned
   and halved
225g (8oz) raspberries
30g (1oz) sugar
100g (3½oz) self-raising flour
15g (½oz) ground almonds
¼ teaspoon baking powder
pinch of salt

½ teaspoon cinnamon
pinch of grated fresh nutmeg
1½ tablespoons golden caster
   sugar, plus extra sugar for
   dusting
1 teaspoon vanilla extract
2 tablespoons corn oil
4 tablespoons soya milk

Preheat the oven to 200°C/400°F/Gas 6. Put the apricots, raspberries and sugar in a saucepan with 1 tablespoon water and cook gently for about 3 minutes until soft. Pour into an ovenproof serving dish. Set aside.

Sift the flour, almonds, baking powder, salt, cinnamon and nutmeg into a bowl. Stir in the golden caster sugar. Make a well in the middle of the dry ingredients. Mix the vanilla, oil and milk and pour the liquid into the well. Mix well, drawing the dry ingredients into the liquid with a wooden spoon. Do not beat. The mixture should be of a 'dropping' consistency. Drop 10 dessertspoonfuls of the mixture on top of the fruit, and dust with a little golden caster sugar. Bake for 30–40 minutes until the scones are risen and golden. Serve warm.

EACH SERVING CONTAINS
Kcals 275 • Protein 6g • Fat 8.5g (of which saturated 1g) • Carbohydrate 46g
Fibre 5g • Kcals from fat 28% • Good source of vitamin C

Crispy Cinnamon Bread Knots with Apricot Sauce

This is a pudding that is loved by everyone, especially children. Make the bread knots when you have something to do during the couple of hours the dough will take to rise. Rising time apart, it won't take long to prepare and cook them.

Serves 6–8

Preparation time: 20 minutes, plus 2 hours rising time
Cooking time: 30 minutes, cooked in batches

280g (10oz) plain flour

2 teaspoons ground cinnamon, plus extra for dusting

½ teaspoon freshly grated nutmeg

2 tablespoons golden caster sugar

pinch of salt

1 sachet (6g) easy blend yeast

1 teaspoon vanilla extract

corn oil, for deep-frying

golden icing sugar, for dusting

For the apricot sauce

100g (3½oz) golden caster sugar

juice of 2 oranges

450g (1lb) dried apricots

2 tablespoons amaretto liqueur

♦ Sift the flour, cinnamon, nutmeg, sugar and salt into a bowl. Make a well in the middle and stir in the yeast and vanilla extract. Gradually pour in 150–200ml (5–7fl oz) tepid water – enough to make a soft dough. As you pour the water in, use a wooden spoon to bring the flour into it from around the edges. You may find it easier to use your hands towards the end of the process. Transfer the dough to a floured surface and knead it with your fingers and the palm of your hand for about 10–15 minutes until it is soft and elastic. Put the dough in a covered bowl and leave to rise in a warm place for about 2 hours until it is 3 or 4 times its original size.

♦ Meanwhile, make the apricot sauce: Put the sugar and orange juice in a saucepan with 4 tablespoons water and heat gently until the sugar has dissolved. Add the apricots, cover and simmer for 10–15 minutes until the fruit is plump and soft. Pour the contents of the saucepan into a food processor, add the liqueur and process to a coarse purée. Stir in enough water to make a smooth sauce. Pour the sauce into a saucepan. Warm the sauce gently when you are ready to serve the bread knots.

♦ When the dough has risen, half-fill a deep-fryer or heavy-based deep saucepan with the corn oil and heat to 190°C (375°F). To test the temperature, drop a cube of bread in the oil – it should brown within

1 minute. Knead the dough again until it is smooth and even. Grease your hands with a little oil and pinch off small pieces of dough. Roll the pieces into 12–15cm (5–6in) lengths and tie each length into a knot. Drop 2–3 knots into the hot oil. Fry them, turning them frequently, for 2–4 minutes until golden brown and puffy. Drain on kitchen paper. Repeat with the remaining knots. Dust with icing sugar and cinnamon and serve immediately with the warm apricot sauce as an accompaniment.

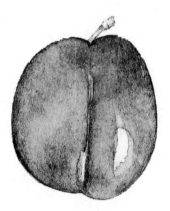

EACH SERVING CONTAINS
6 servings: Kcals 514 • Protein 8g • Fat 14g (of which saturated 1g)
Carbohydrate 93g • Fibre 7g • Kcals from fat 24%
8 servings: Kcals 385 • Protein 6g • Fat 10g (of which saturated 1g)
Carbohydrate 44g • Fibre 5g • Kcals from fat 24%

menus

When you are planning a menu the nutritional balance of each course is just the start. Flavours, colours and textures of the food all need to be considered. The courses must be both complementary and contrasting. You will also have to consider the time available for preparation and cooking, and the kind of meal you want to serve.

A Supper Party

◆

Choose dishes that can be doubled or trebled to accommodate the
number of guests. The menu needs to be relaxed and casual but still
impressive. The preparation should be done before your guests arrive.

Make a selection of 'nibbles' that can be put in bowls and dotted
around the room so that people can eat as and when they choose:

Cayenne chips, Hot and spicy popcorn, Coriander spiced nuts
Serve the cayenne chips first. If you serve hot and cold nibbles at the
same time guests may leave the hot food until it has gone cold.

◆

Juma's African curry
Tuscan tarts

◆

Chocolate raspberry hazelnut cake
Serve with a big bowl of crushed raspberries
Treacle tart

A Supper to Prepare Ahead

◆

This is a menu for those occasions when you have friends staying with
you and you want to take them out for the day but also want to serve
them a delicious supper in the evening. Prepare these dishes the day
before and simply heat and assemble them when you are ready to eat.
Melon with toasted seeds

◆

Pacific Rim coconut curry

◆

Moroccan spiced rice pudding

Sunday Lunch

◆

The emphasis here is food for all the family. You want everyone to be relaxed and happy and to enjoy the day. Time is not as important as it often is during the week, so you can serve a meal that may take a while to cook or prepare – but get everyone in to the kitchen to help.

Roasted apple, onion and potato soup
Serve with parsley and garlic pitta toasts

◆

Vegan lasagne
Serve with a fresh green salad

◆

Pecan and butternut squash tart *or*
Coconut ice dessert with chocolate ripple

Romantic Meal for Two

◆

Food is sensual. For this light, but very satisfying, menu I have chosen food that you can eat with your hands or feed to each other.

Baked asparagus with garlic croutons

◆

Vegan sushi with pickled ginger and soy

◆

Orange and passionfruit sorbet *or*
Fresh fruits in wine with fresh basil

A Dinner for His/Her Parents

◆

Planning and preparation are the key to a successful dinner party –
even more so when you want to impress your guests. Choose dishes
that can be made in advance, allowing you to relax and entertain your
guests without having to worry about the food.

Creamy carrot and ginger soup
Serve with crispy curls of toast

◆

Moroccan-style chick peas with saffron rice

◆

Plum and cinnamon crisp

A Quick Lunch

◆

There are always occasions when we want to invite friends for lunch
on Saturday, but don't want to spend hours preparing the food. This
menu is perfect for those situations. The flapjacks can be made in
advance and frozen until needed. If you are lucky enough to have
good weather, food like this can be enjoyed in the garden.

Puréed chick peas with griddled vegetables

◆

Bright red pepper linguine

◆

Banana flapjacks with fresh fruit compote

A Picnic

◆

All the following recipes are quick to prepare and easy to transport: take the gazpacho in a Thermos flask and put the croutons and the salad or sandwiches in separate picnic boxes or containers. Don't forget the pepper mill for the strawberries and black pepper.

Spicy gazpacho soup with paprika croutons

◆

Summer pasta salad *or*
Thai vegetables in fresh herb bread

◆

Strawberries with black pepper

A Special Event

◆

A wonderful dish of wild mushrooms with crushed red peppercorns and garlic is a fabulous way to start a celebratory meal. The lemon sherbert will clear the palate before you serve the impressive golden onion tarts.

Mushrooms with peppercorns and garlic

◆

Lemon sherbert cups (without the crushed blueberries)

◆

Sticky golden onion tarts

◆

Fruits with cardamom and vanilla

index

almonds: caramelized peach and almond tart, 174
  Moroccan spiced rice pudding, 155
  roasted baby courgettes, 18
apples: apple and pear crisp, 172
  beetroot with vinaigrette, 36
  roasted apple, onion and sweet potato soup, 45–6
  walnut layer with apple and brandy sauce, 179
apricots: apricot and raspberry cobbler, 183
  crispy cinnamon bread knots with apricot sauce, 184–5
  poached fruits in lavender-infused syrup with toffee crisps, 158
asparagus: baked asparagus with garlic croutons, 33
  puréed chick peas with griddled vegetables, 31
  Thai noodles with chilli and lemon grass dressing, 105
aubergines: aubergine and potato bake, 137
  aubergine butter with sea salt crusted potatoes, 136
  aubergine slices with lemon and fresh coriander, 135
  griddled aubergines with black olive dressing, 81
  Pacific Rim coconut curry, 139–40
  warm tomato and aubergine stacks, 74
avocados: avocado butter with tomato relish in focaccia, 94
  puréed avocado dip with pickled ginger and wasabi, 20
  salad of ciabatta croutons with avocado, grapefruit and vinaigrette, 87
  vegan sushi with avocado and cucumber, 107
  with beans and coriander, 44

baby Mediterranean tarts with fresh basil purée, 40
balsamic white peach salad with parsley shortcakes, 78–9
balti, 131–2
bananas: baked bananas with orange and hazelnuts, 177
  banana flapjacks with fresh fruit compote, 178
basil: baby Mediterranean tarts with fresh basil purée, 40
  corn, coconut, lime and basil soup, 49–50
  fresh fruits in wine with, 167
  fresh ginger and basil pasta, 63
  fried tomato toasts, 41
  roasted garlic polenta with sautéed tomatoes, 99
  tomato and basil risotto, 108
bean sprouts: chillied spring rolls with a dipping sauce, 119
beans: avocado with beans and coriander, 44
  fresh broad beans with paprika and lemon, 82
  maize with, 115
  potatoes with broad beans and mint vinaigrette, 43
  purée of beans and potatoes with olive oil, 70

stir-fried black beans with lime and chilli, 133

warm butter bean purée, 32

warm lemon and olive oil beans on rosemary mash, 75

beetroot: beetroot with vinaigrette, 36

vegetable crisps, 22

vivid beetroot and horseradish gnocchi, 67

berries, 11

black beans, stir-fried with lime and chilli, 133

blood oranges with red onions, black olives and fennel dressing, 42

blueberries, lemon sherbert cups with, 163

borlotti beans: warm lemon and olive oil beans on rosemary mash, 75

brazil nuts: banana flapjacks with fresh fruit compote, 178

bread, 11

avocado butter with tomato relish in focaccia, 94

baked asparagus with garlic croutons, 33

carrots with pomegranate syrup in pitta breads, 95

crispy cinnamon bread knots with apricot sauce, 184–5

crunchy Marmite toasts, 30

four-onion croustades, 73

fried tomato toasts, 41

paprika croutons, 54

parsley and garlic pitta toasts, 30

pitta breads with garlic cream and fresh lime, 92

rich mushrooms on toast with truffle oil, 37

salad of ciabatta croutons with avocado, grapefruit and vinaigrette, 87

spicy pitta toasts, 30

spicy satay on white bread, 88

Thai vegetables in fresh herb bread, 93

broad beans, 11

fresh broad beans with paprika and lemon, 82

potatoes with broad beans and mint vinaigrette, 43

butter bean purée, warm, 32

butternut squash: pecan and butternut squash tart, 175

roasted squash soup with fresh coriander, 52

cakes: chocolate raspberry hazelnut cake, 181

sponge cake with strawberries and lemon balm, 180

calcium, 5

canned food, 6

cannellini beans: avocado with beans and coriander, 44

caramelized fennel and shallot risotto, 109

caramelized oranges with cranberries, 170

caramelized peach and almond tart, 174

carbohydrates, 5

cardamom, fruits with cardamom and vanilla, 159

carrots: creamy carrot and ginger soup with curly toasts, 51

puréed chick peas with griddled vegetables, 31

with pomegranate syrup in pitta breads, 95

cashew nuts: coriander spiced nuts, 16

cayenne chips, 23

cheese: vegan lasagne, 147–8

cherry jam, orange custards with, 171

chestnuts, roasted potatoes and parsnips with chestnuts and sage, 85

chick peas: Moroccan spiced couscous with fruits, 59

Moroccan spiced red potato with chick peas, 129

Moroccan-style chick peas with saffron rice, 145

puréed chick peas with griddled vegetables, 31

chick-pea batter, vegetables in crispy, 29–30

chillies, 10

bright red pepper pesto linguine, 62

chilli and coriander sweetcorn fritters, 83–4

chilli pakoras with chunky tomato chutney, 26–7

chillied spring rolls with a dipping sauce, 119

crunchy baked tomatoes with lime, onion and chilli, 39

Thai green vegetable curry, 134

Thai noodles with chilli and lemon grass dressing, 105

wontons with chilli sauce, 118

chips, cayenne, 23

chocolate: chocolate raspberry hazelnut cake, 181

coconut ice dessert with chocolate sauce, 164–5

chutneys: chunky tomato, 143–4

peach and lemon grass, 127–8

ciabatta: salad of ciabatta croutons with avocado, grapefruit and vinaigrette, 87

cinnamon bread knots with apricot sauce, 184–5

cobbler, apricot and raspberry, 183

coconut cream: papaya and coconut sherbert, 162

spicy vegetables and coconut cream, 114

coconut milk: coconut ice dessert with chocolate sauce, 164–5

coconut rice pudding with mango and papaya, 154

corn, coconut, lime and basil soup, 49–50

Malaysian vegetables, 125

Pacific Rim coconut curry, 139–40

Thai pumpkin and coconut soup, 47

coriander leaves: aubergine slices with lemon and, 135

avocado with beans and, 44

chilli and coriander sweetcorn fritters, 83–4

griddled vegetables on lemon grass sticks with coriander basmati, 122–3 new potatoes and petit pois with pungent green sauce, 146

papaya and coriander salsa on coconut rice, 80

roasted squash soup with, 52

tomato soup with coriander salsa, 48

coriander seeds: coriander spiced nuts, 16

warm cumin and coriander spinach on garlic mash, 76

corn: avocado with beans and coriander, 44

chilli and coriander sweetcorn fritters with tomato sauce, 83–4

corn, coconut, lime and basil soup, 49–50

hot and spicy popcorn, 17

puréed chick peas with griddled vegetables, 31

summer pasta salad, 65

courgettes: crispy polenta peppers and courgettes with balsamic vinegar, 138

roasted baby courgettes, 18

couscous: griddled red onion slices with, 60

Moroccan spiced couscous with fruits, 59

roasted vegetables with couscous and lemon pepper oil, 124

warm couscous with garlic, black olives and tomatoes, 61

cranberries, caramelized oranges with, 170

crisps, vegetable, 22

croustades, four-onion, 73

croutons: ciabatta, 87

garlic, 33

paprika, 54

cucumber, vegan sushi with avocado and, 107

cumin and coriander spinach on garlic mash, 76

curries: Juma's special African curry, 116–17

Pacific Rim coconut curry, 139–40

Thai green vegetable curry, 134

custards, orange with cherry jam, 171

desserts, 151–85

dinner party menus, 190–1

dips: lemon tahini, 21

puréed avocado with pickled ginger and wasabi, 20

warm butter bean purée, 32

dried fruit, 6

Moroccan spiced couscous with fruits, 59

fat, 5

fennel: blood oranges with red onions, black olives and fennel dressing, 42

caramelized fennel and shallot risotto, 109

fennel and ginger tarts, 72

figs, toffee, 169

flapjacks, banana, 178

focaccia, avocado butter with tomato relish in, 94

four-onion croustades, 73

freezers, 11

fridges, 9–11
fritters, chilli and coriander
    sweetcorn, 83–4
frozen yogurt crunch with raspberry
    sauce, 166
fruit: banana flapjacks with fresh
    fruit compote, 178
    fresh fruits in wine with basil,
      167
    fruits with cardamom and vanilla,
      159
    winter fruit salad, 182
    see also apples, raspberries etc

galette, Mediterranean, 71
garlic: aubergine and potato bake,
    137
    aubergine butter with sea salt
      crusted potatoes, 136
    baked asparagus with garlic
      croutons, 33
    homemade pizzas, 149–50
    parsley and garlic pitta toasts, 30
    pitta breads with garlic cream and
      fresh lime, 92
    roasted garlic and walnut
      linguine, 104
    roasted garlic polenta with
      sautéed tomatoes, 99
    warm couscous with garlic, black
      olives and tomatoes, 61
    warm cumin and coriander
      spinach on garlic mash, 76
    winter green salad with very
      garlicky vinaigrette, 90
    with peppercorns and garlic, 38
gazpacho soup with paprika
    croutons, 54

ginger, 10
    baked pears and ginger, 156
    creamy carrot and ginger soup,
      51
    fennel and ginger tarts, 72
    fresh ginger and basil pasta, 63
ginger, pickled, 12
    puréed avocado dip with pickled
      ginger and wasabi, 20
gnocchi: with tomatoes and fresh
    mint, 101
    vivid beetroot and horseradish
      gnocchi, 67
grains, 7
grapefruit, salad of ciabatta
    croutons with avocado,
    grapefruit and vinaigrette, 87

hazelnuts: baked bananas with
    orange and, 177
    chocolate raspberry hazelnut
      cake, 181
    coriander spiced nuts, 16
    warm hazelnut scones with fruit
      salsa, 153
herbs, 10
homemade pizzas, 149–50
honey, 12
horseradish: vivid beetroot and
    horseradish gnocchi, 67

ice-cream, 11
    baked bananas with orange and
      hazelnuts, 177
    coconut ice dessert with
      chocolate sauce, 164–5
Indian vegetables, 130
ingredients, 6–12

iron, 4–5

jams, 7
  cherry jam, 171
Japanese rice bowl with vegetables, 111
Juma's special African curry, 116–17

kaffir lime leaves, 12
kidney beans: maize with beans, 115

lasagne, vegan, 147–8
leeks: four-onion croustades, 73
  sticky golden onion tarts, 120
lemon, 10
  aubergine slices with lemon and fresh coriander, 135
  fresh broad beans with paprika and, 82
  lemon sherbert cups with crushed blueberries, 163
  lemon tahini dip, 21
  warm lemon and olive oil beans on rosemary mash, 75
lemon balm, sponge cake with strawberries and, 180
lemon grass, 10
  griddled vegetables on lemon grass sticks with coriander basmati, 122–3
  peach and lemon grass chutney, 127–8
  Thai noodles with chilli and lemon grass dressing, 105
lime, 10
  corn, coconut, lime and basil soup, 49–50
  crunchy baked tomatoes with lime, onion and chilli, 39
  pitta breads with garlic cream and fresh lime, 92
linguine: bright red pepper pesto, 62
  roasted garlic and walnut, 104
  tomato and pine nut linguine with caramelized lemon, 100
lunch menus, 190–1

main courses, 97–150
maize with beans, 115
Malaysian vegetables, 125
mango: coconut rice pudding with mango and papaya, 154
margarine, vegan, 10–11
Marmite toasts, crunchy, 30
Mediterranean galette, 71
Mediterranean potatoes with olives, herbs and tomatoes, 126
Mediterranean tarts with fresh basil purée, 40
melon: with red wine and mint sauce, 24
  with toasted seeds, 25
menus, 187–92
minerals, 3–5
mint: gnocchi with tomatoes and, 101
  melon with red wine and mint sauce, 24
  potatoes with broad beans and mint vinaigrette, 43
Moroccan pilaff, 110
Moroccan spiced couscous with fruits, 59

Moroccan spiced red potato with chick peas, 129
Moroccan spiced rice pudding, 155
Moroccan-style chick peas with saffron rice, 145
mushrooms: baked asparagus with garlic croutons, 33
balti, 131–2
individual crispy porcini bakes, 142
mixed mushrooms and tofu pasta, 102
rich mushroom sauce with tagliatelle, 66
rich mushrooms on toast with truffle oil, 37
vegan lasagne, 147–8
wild mushroom soup, 53
with peppercorns and garlic, 38
wontons with chilli sauce, 118

nectarine and berry crisp, 172
noodles: red cabbage with sake on rice noodles, 106
Thai noodles with chilli and lemon grass dressing, 105
Thai pumpkin and coconut soup, 47
nutrition, 3–6
nuts, 7
nut spreads, 7
spiced nuts, 15
see also almonds, walnuts etc

oats: banana flapjacks, 178
oils, 7
olives: baby Mediterranean tarts with fresh basil purée, 40

balsamic white peach salad, 78–9
griddled aubergines with black olive dressing, 81
Mediterranean potatoes with olives, herbs and tomatoes, 126
warm couscous with garlic, black olives and tomatoes, 61
with fresh rosemary and orange, 19
onions: blood oranges with red onions, black olives and fennel dressing, 42
four-onion croustades, 73
griddled red onion slices with couscous, 60
roasted apple, onion and sweet potato soup, 45–6
roasted red onions and wilted spinach with sweet potatoes, 141
sticky golden onion tarts, 120
see also spring onions
oranges: baked bananas with oranges and hazelnuts, 177
blood oranges with red onions, black olives and fennel dressing, 42
caramelized oranges with cranberries, 170
orange and passion fruit sorbet, 160–1
orange custards with cherry jam, 171
strawberries with black pepper, 168

Pacific Rim coconut curry, 139–40

pak choi, steamed with soy sauce and toasted seeds, 28

pakoras, chilli, 26–7

pancakes, 173

papaya: coconut rice pudding with mango and, 154

papaya and coconut sherbert, 162

papaya and coriander salsa on coconut rice, 80

paprika: fresh broad beans with paprika and lemon, 82

paprika croutons, 54

parsley: parsley and garlic pitta toasts, 30

parsley shortcakes, 78–9

red cabbage relish with parsley mash, 77

parsnips: roasted potatoes and parsnips with chestnuts and sage, 85

vegetable crisps, 22

passion fruit and orange sorbet, 160–1

pasta, 7

bright red pepper pesto linguine, 62

fresh ginger and basil pasta, 63

individual crispy porcini bakes, 142

mixed mushrooms and tofu pasta, 102

rich mushroom sauce with tagliatelle, 66

roast vine tomatoes and pasta, 64

roasted garlic and walnut linguine, 104

spaghetti with tomato sauce, 103

summer pasta salad, 65

tomato and pine nut linguine with caramelized lemon, 100

vegan lasagne, 147–8

pastes, 8

pastries: samosas with mango chutney, 68–9

pastry, 11

peaches: balsamic white peach salad, 78–9

caramelized peach and almond tart, 174

peach and lemon grass chutney, 127–8

poached fruits in lavender-infused syrup with toffee crisps, 158

peanut butter: spicy satay on white bread, 88

pears: apple and pear crisp, 172

baked pears and ginger, 156

hot poached pears with toffee crisps, 157

very modern Waldorf salad, 91

peas see petits pois

pecan and butternut squash tart, 175

penne: individual crispy porcini bakes, 142

pepper: strawberries with black pepper, 168

peppercorns: mushrooms with peppercorns and garlic, 38

peppers: bright red pepper pesto linguine, 62

crispy polenta peppers and courgettes with balsamic vinegar, 138

Tuscan tarts, 121
pesto: bright red pepper pesto
    linguine, 62
petits pois, 11
    new potatoes and petits pois with
    pungent green sauce, 146
picnics, 192
pilaff, Moroccan, 110
pine nuts: tomato and pine nut
    linguine, 100
pitta breads: carrots with
    pomegranate syrup in, 95
    parsley and garlic pitta toasts, 30
    spicy pitta toasts, 30
    with garlic cream and fresh lime,
    92
pizzas, homemade, 149–50
plum and cinnamon crisp, 172
polenta: crispy polenta peppers and
    courgettes with balsamic
    vinegar, 138
    roasted garlic polenta with
    sautéed tomatoes, 99
pomegranate syrup, carrots in pitta
    breads with, 95
popcorn, hot and spicy, 17
potatoes: aubergine and potato
    bake, 137
    aubergine butter with sea salt
    crusted potatoes, 136
    cayenne chips, 23
    Mediterranean potatoes with
    olives, herbs and tomatoes,
    126
    Moroccan spiced red potato with
    chick peas, 129
    new potatoes and petits pois with
    pungent green sauce, 146

Pacific Rim coconut curry,
    139–40
potato cakes with peach and
    lemon grass chutney, 127–8
purée of beans and potatoes with
    olive oil, 70
red cabbage relish with parsley
    mash, 77
roasted potatoes and parsnips
    with chestnuts and sage, 85
samosas with mango chutney,
    68–9
Spanish potato gratin, 86
warm cumin and coriander
    spinach on garlic mash, 76
warm lemon and olive oil beans
    on rosemary mash, 75
with broad beans and mint
    vinaigrette, 43
proteins, 5–6
pulses, 8
pumpkin and coconut soup, Thai,
    47
pumpkin seeds: melon with toasted
    seeds, 25
    steamed pak choi with soy sauce
    and toasted seeds, 28

raisins: a very modern Waldorf
    salad, 91
raspberries: apricot and raspberry
    cobbler, 183
    chocolate raspberry hazelnut
    cake, 181
    frozen yogurt crunch with
    raspberry sauce, 166
    nectarine and berry crisp, 172
    warm hazelnut scones with fruit

salsa, 153
red cabbage: red cabbage relish
    with parsley mash, 77
  with sake on rice noodles, 106
red rice salad, 89
relishes: red cabbage, 77
  tomato, 94
rice, 8
  caramelized fennel and shallot
      risotto, 109
  coconut rice pudding with mango
      and papaya, 154
  griddled vegetables on lemon
      grass sticks with coriander
      basmati, 122–3
  Indian vegetables, 130
  Japanese rice bowl with
      vegetables, 111
  Moroccan pilaff, 110
  Moroccan spiced rice pudding,
      155
  Moroccan-style chick peas with
      saffron rice, 145
  papaya and coriander salsa on
      coconut rice, 80
  red rice salad, 89
  spicy vegetables and coconut
      cream, 114
  spring vegetables with saffron
      basmati rice, 112–13
  Thai green vegetable curry, 134
  tomato and basil risotto, 108
  vegan sushi with avocado and
      cucumber, 107
risotto see rice
rocket: balsamic white peach salad,
    78–9
  homemade pizzas, 149–50

romantic menu, 190
rosemary: homemade pizzas,
    149–50
  olives with fresh rosemary and
      orange, 19
  warm lemon and olive oil beans
      on rosemary mash, 75

saffron: Moroccan-style chick peas
      with saffron rice, 145
  spring vegetables with saffron
      and basmati rice, 112–13
sage, roasted potatoes and parsnips
    with chestnuts and, 85
salads: balsamic white peach salad,
    78–9
  ciabatta croutons with avocado,
      grapefruit and vinaigrette, 87
  red rice salad, 89
  summer pasta salad, 65
  very modern Waldorf salad, 91
  winter green salad with very
      garlicky vinaigrette, 90
salsas, 10
  coriander, 48
  fruit, 153
  papaya and coriander, 80
  watercress, 34–5
salt, 8
samosas with mango chutney, 68–9
satay on white bread, 88
sauces, 8
scones, warm hazelnut, 153
seaweed, 8
seeds, 7
sesame seeds: coriander spiced
      nuts, 16
  crunchy Marmite toasts, 30

sherbert: lemon sherbert cups with crushed blueberries, 163
papaya and coconut sherbert, 162
shortcakes, parsley, 78–9
snacks and light meals, 57–95
sorbets, 11
orange and passion fruit, 160–1
soups, 45–54
corn, coconut, lime and basil, 49–50
creamy carrot and ginger, 51
roasted apple, onion and sweet potato, 45–6
roasted squash with fresh coriander, 52
spicy gazpacho with paprika croutons, 54
Thai pumpkin and coconut, 47
tomato soup with coriander salsa, 48
wild mushroom, 53
soy sauce, steamed pak choi with soy sauce and toasted seeds, 28
soya cream, 10
soya milk, 10
Moroccan spiced rice pudding, 155
spaghetti with tomato sauce, 103
Spanish potato gratin, 86
spiced nuts, 15
spices, 8–9
spicy pitta toasts, 30
spinach: roasted red onions and wilted spinach with sweet potatoes, 141
vegan lasagne, 147–8

warm cumin and coriander spinach on garlic mash, 76
spirits, 12
sponge cake with strawberries and lemon balm, 180
spring onions: crunchy baked tomatoes with lime, onion and chilli, 39
spring rolls, chillied, 119
spring vegetables with saffron basmati rice, 112–13
squash: pecan and butternut squash tart, 175
roasted squash soup with fresh coriander, 52
starters, 13–44
sticky golden onion tarts, 120
stock, vegetable, 9, 55
strawberries: sponge cake with strawberries and lemon balm, 180
with black pepper, 168
sugar, 9
sugarsnap peas: summer pasta salad, 65
summer pasta salad, 65
Sunday lunch, 190
supper menus, 189
sushi with avocado and cucumber, 107
sweet potatoes: hot griddled sweet potato with watercress salsa, 34–5
roasted apple, onion and sweet potato soup, 45–6
roasted red onions and wilted spinach with, 141
vegetable crisps, 22

sweetcorn *see* corn

tagliatelle, rich mushroom sauce with, 66
tahini dip, lemon, 21
tarts: baby Mediterranean tarts with fresh basil purée, 40
caramelized peach and almond tart, 174
fennel and ginger tarts, 72
pecan and butternut squash tart, 175
sticky golden onion tarts, 120
treacle tart, 176
Tuscan tarts, 121
Thai green vegetable curry, 134
Thai noodles with chilli and lemon grass dressing, 105
Thai pumpkin and coconut soup, 47
Thai vegetables in fresh herb bread, 93
toasts: crunchy Marmite toasts, 30
curly toasts, 51
fried tomato toasts, 41
parsley and garlic pitta toasts, 30
rich mushrooms on toast with truffle oil, 37
spicy pitta toasts, 30
toffee crisps: hot poached pears with, 157
poached fruits in lavender-infused syrup with, 158
toffee figs with a glass of brandy, 169
tofu: mixed mushrooms and tofu pasta, 102
wild mushroom soup, 53

tomatoes: aubergine and potato bake, 137
avocado butter with tomato relish in focaccia, 94
avocado with beans and coriander, 44
chilli and coriander sweetcorn fritters with tomato sauce, 83–4
crunchy baked tomatoes with lime, onion and chilli, 39
fried tomato toasts, 41
gnocchi with tomatoes and fresh mint, 101
homemade pizzas, 149–50
hot griddled sweet potato with watercress salsa, 34–5
Mediterranean potatoes with olives, herbs and tomatoes, 126
Moroccan spiced red potato with chick peas, 129
roast vine tomatoes and pasta, 64
roasted garlic polenta with sautéed tomatoes, 99
spaghetti with tomato sauce, 103
Spanish potato gratin, 86
spicy gazpacho soup with paprika croutons, 54
spicy vegetable rounds with chunky tomato chutney, 143–4
summer pasta salad, 65
tomato and basil risotto, 108
tomato and pine nut linguine with caramelized lemon, 100
tomato soup with coriander salsa,

48

Tuscan tarts, 121

vegan lasagne, 147–8

warm couscous with garlic, black olives and tomatoes, 61

warm tomato and aubergine stacks, 74

tortillas: stir-fried black beans with lime and chilli, 133

toffee crisps, 157

treacle tart, 176

truffle oil, rich mushrooms on toast with, 37

Tuscan tarts, 121

vegan sushi with avocado and cucumber, 107

vegetables, 11

chilli pakoras with chunky tomato chutney, 26–7

griddled vegetables on lemon grass sticks with coriander basmati, 122–3

Indian vegetables, 130

Japanese rice bowl with vegetables, 111

Juma's special African curry, 116–17

Malaysian vegetables, 125

Mediterranean galette, 71

puréed chick peas with griddled vegetables, 31

roasted vegetables with couscous and lemon pepper oil, 124

spicy vegetable rounds with chunky tomato chutney, 143–4

spicy vegetables and coconut cream, 114

spring vegetables with saffron basmati rice, 112–13

Thai green vegetable curry, 134

Thai vegetables in fresh herb bread, 93

vegetable crisps, 22

vegetable stock, 9, 55

vegetables in a crispy chick-pea batter, 29–30

very modern Waldorf salad, 91

vinaigrette: beetroot with, 36

mint, 43

very garlicky, 90

vinegars, 9

vitamin B12, 4

vitamin D, 4

vitamins, 3–4

vivid beetroot and horseradish gnocchi, 67

walnuts: roasted garlic and walnut linguine, 104

very modern Waldorf salad, 91

walnut layer with apple and brandy sauce, 179

wasabi, 12

puréed avocado dip with pickled ginger and, 20

watercress: hot griddled sweet potato with watercress salsa, 34–5

warm lemon and olive oil beans on rosemary mash, 75

white beans: purée of beans and potatoes with olive oil, 70

wines, 12

fresh fruits in wine with basil,

167
melon with red wine and mint
    sauce, 24
winter fruit salad, 182
winter green salad with very
    garlicky vinaigrette, 90

wontons with chilli sauce, 118

yogurt: frozen yogurt crunch with
    raspberry sauce, 166

ORDER FORM

CARDAMOM & CORIANDER
by Simon Morris

Simon Morris, winner of the 1997 National Curry Chef competition, reveals the secrets of authentic Indian cookery, reinvented with a contemporary twist in his first book, *Cardamom & Coriander*. In over 100 recipes, he draws on first-hand experience from his regular trips to research the flavours, ingredients and techniques of the country – prising recipes from street vendors and top chefs alike. Dishes range from the simple – Aromatic Turkey and Guava and Lime Sorbet – to spectacular dishes such as Venison Rogon Josh and the prize-winning dish of Hyderabadi Lamb with Rice and Peas. One of the beauties of Indian cooking, especially for a dinner party, is that all the work can be done ahead of time, leaving you to sit with your guests and enjoy the evening. Whether you want to concoct a simple yet delicious after-work meal for two, or something more lavish for entertaining, this book is for you.

**£17.99, ISBN 1 900512 48 3, 224pp, 234x153mm, hardback,
8 pp colour photographs**

TO ORDER: ring your local bookshop or our freefone credit card
hotline on 0500 418 419

ORDER FORM

REAL FAST VEGETARIAN FOOD
by Ursula Ferrigno

For too long vegetarian food has conjured up images of heavy,
wholemeal food and 'worthy-but-dull' recipes. Now, Ursula
Ferrigno's *Real Fast Vegetarian Food* reinvents vegetarian cooking
to show how anybody can create delicious, colourful and
inspirational food with the minimum of fuss.

Choose from 150 recipes ranging from Wild Mushroom and Basil
Tart to Giant Stuffed Mushrooms to The Richest Chocolate
Cake Ever.

Written with passion for the freshest of ingredients and quality extra
virgin olive oils, this is the guide to modern vegetarian cooking.

£8.99, ISBN 1 900512 13 0, 224pp, paperback, 216x135mm

TO ORDER: ring your local bookshop or our freefone credit card
hotline on 0500 418 419

ORDER FORM

URSULA'S ITALIAN CAKES AND DESSERTS
by Ursula Ferrigno

Choose from the best of Italian family cooking with Ursula's Italian-inspired pastries, cakes, puddings – and more. Written with a passion for fresh ingredients and seasonal produce, *Ursula's Italian Cakes and Desserts* draws on recipes handed down by her Italian grandmother, family and friends – recipes tourists never hear of!

Select from 120 recipes ranging from apricot and almond tart to warm plum and hazelnut cake, from chocolate ice-cream to orange and almond cookies, from apple and rosemary cake to moist cherry cake.

All are straightforward to prepare and aimed at cooks of all standards. Whether you are looking for a simple dessert for a family meal or something a little more special for entertaining friends, this is the definitive guide to the famous Italian 'dolce'.

£8.99, ISBN 1 900512 27 0, 224pp, 216x135mm, paperback, 8 pages colour photographs

---

TO ORDER: ring your local bookshop or our freefone credit card hotline on 0500 418 419

ORDER FORM

COOK ORGANIC
by Gilli Davies

Does your roast chicken taste bland and your tomatoes have no flavour? Are you worried about BSE, Salmonella and E-coli? Does the way food is produced, processed and packed with additives cause you increasing concern? The answer is simple – cook organic!

With organic products of all kinds now widely available, organic cooking has finally come of age. Ordinary modern cookbooks do not take account of the different methods required to deal with the intense flavours of organic ingredients. *Cook Organic* is the first to bring to busy people the possibility of enjoying wonderful flavours from the best of naturally produced foods.

Gone is the 'sandals and beads' hippy image of organic food. The modern organic cookery is stylish and delicious, with 150 recipes here ranging from Fennel and Lemongrass Soup to Squid in Red Wine, Smoked Duck with Strawberry Vinaigrette, Broccoli and Blue Cheese Soufflés, Tagine of Lamb with Couscous and Mango and Lime Ice Cream. Endorsed by the Soil Association, this book explains why organic food really is different, and includes a section on organic ingredients and a list of organic mail-order suppliers. *Cook Organic* is written with a passion for fresh ingredients and no-fuss cooking to help you create food that is good for you and good for the planet.

£8.99, ISBN 1 900512 36 X, 208pp, 216x135mm, paperback

TO ORDER: ring your local bookshop or our freefone credit card hotline on 0500 418 419

ORDER FORM

ALDO'S ITALIAN FOOD FOR FRIENDS
by Aldo Zilli

Drawing on the traditions of his native Italian cookery, Aldo Zilli has created a light and stylish cuisine which is as achievable in the home as in the kitchens of his renowned Soho restaurants.

The hallmark of the recipes in *Aldo's Italian Food for Friends* is a combination of simplicity and flair, presented with Aldo's unique sense of fun and zest for living. Choose from 150 recipes ranging from simple starters such as Stuffed Focaccia to spectacular pastas such as Aldo's special Spaghetti with Lobster, and creamy risottos made with wild mushrooms, fennel or asparagus and mascarpone. Desserts to die for include Baby Chocolate Tarts with Vanilla Cream and Fruits of the Forest Tiramisù.

Aldo's dishes are aimed at all levels of cook and are accompanied by a glossary of cooking terms and advice on ingredients and wines to help you achieve authentic Italian results and ensure that you are ready to rustle up something stunning for friends at a moment's notice.

Whether you are cooking for an intimate supper or a Christmas lunch, Aldo's Italian Food for Friends will impress your guests and introduce them to traditional Italian hospitality with a modern touch.

£12.99, ISBN 1 900512 35 1, 240pp, 246x189mm, paperback, 16 pages colour photographs

TO ORDER: ring your local bookshop or our freefone credit card hotline on 0500 418 419

AT HOME WITH ROSS BURDEN
by Ross Burden

Many people think they don't have the time or skill to produce a
meal to impress friends, but in this inspiring yet practical book Ross
shows how, with a little effort and imagination, almost anything is
possible. He has a horror of over-fussy creations, and when
entertaining prefers terrines, tarts and oven-to-table dishes,
believing the cook should be back in the dining room where he or
she belongs, surrounded by friends.

Since arriving from his native New Zealand in 1990, Ross Burden
has rapidly become (at the age of 29) Britain's most stylish new
chef. A veteran of *Ready, Steady Cook*, Ross has also displayed
his talents on his own show on the Carlton Food Network, as well
as many other programmes. Running his own catering company
has given him the experience of entertaining for every type
of occasion.

The mouth-watering recipes in this book reflect Ross's passionate
belief in cooking with fresh seasonal ingredients. His love of travel
is reflected in the flavours and culinary traditions he has drawn from
every corner of the globe – from Thai fish cakes with lime leaf and
coriander dip, loin of lamb with Moroccan spices and couscous, to
poached pear with spun sugar and lime caramel sauce.

So whether you're planning a big party celebration, or just having a
few close friends round for a fun evening, *At Home with Ross
Burden* is the perfect companion.

**£12.99, ISBN 1 900512 55 6, 256pp, 246x189mm, paperback,
16 pages colour photographs**